M000020934

Your Cells Are Listening....
What you say matters!

Denae Arias

Copyright © 2018 by Denae Arias

All rights reserved. No part of this book
may be reproduced or used in any
manner without written permission of
the copyright owner except for the use
of quotations in a book review. For
more information, address:
denae@denaearias.com

FIRST EDITION

Illustrations copyright © 2018 by Nico Zamora
Design by Nico Zamora
Cover art by Nico Zamora

ISBN 978-1-7928-8597-6 (*paperback*)

www.denaearias.com

TABLE OF CONTENTS

DEDICATION

I dedicate this book to all the beautiful hearts who are awakening during this exciting time on our planet who are seeking answers, truth and hope. No matter what you are currently facing or what you have been through, life has led you here to this book. Disease, loneliness, lack, heartbreak, anxiety, may you find the strength within yourself to question everything you thought you believed and knew about. Your body, your purpose, and your beliefs that keep you stuck. Let the words within these pages well up from within you and ignite a fire in your heart that inspires you to put the truth to the test and allow yourself the freedom to go for all that you desire.

We were not meant to come to earth to live, die and go to Heaven. No way! We are here to bring heaven on earth.

SPECIAL DEDICATION

Allie, the past few years have tested you beyond what you thought you could handle and each time you come through stronger and changed and I want you to know how proud I am of you and the mother that you are. May you find understanding and love within these pages and the strength and peace to be all that you are meant to be. May you find the love your soul seeks and you experience the peace, grace and freedom you so deserve. I love you.

Without the influences and relationships with the Great Cosmic Beings and Grand Cosmic Hierarchy in my life, this book would not have been.

To Master Teacher Asun whom I call Papa, your guidance, love, butt-kicking, and shenanigans along with all the laughter have made this journey so amazing. My life is so much more than I ever thought it could be since you have entered in such a tangible way. I love you.

To Mother Akasha whom I call Momma, your love consumes me into a beautiful garden of grace, peace, tranquility, and freedom that I longed for. The night you came and revealed yourself to me – from that instant I knew I had found a home. Your radiance was so loving and so unlike anything I have experienced on Earth. I want to share your love and light with the world. Your grace is sufficient and I value living within your grace.

To my Ascended Master Sponsor, the Great Master St. Germain: Thank you for over lighting me, and this work with your instruction, guidance, support, love, and wisdom. Your role in my life is unmistakable and I value all you have taught me. Thank you for keeping me on my toes and blowing my mind all the time. My love for you grows deeper every day and I am humbled, honored and gracious for all the time and experiences with you.

PROLOGUE

Beautiful heart your decision in getting this book was the best investment in yourself you could make. Make sure you are comfortable and ready to settle in and get illumined as you read through these pages. It is time to face yourself.

Life is not linear from A to Z, it is circular, all-encompassing and ever expanding. While truth never changes it does expand and goes deeper at each level. Everything that is truth grows and expands upon itself. At one level, a word can mean one thing; at a deeper level that word or truth will take on a deeper meaning. As you continue to awaken, be open to this deep infinite growth and embrace it. Up until this point, you have been living life from a linear finite perspective. Open up your mind and heart and allow the energy to flow.

INTRODUCTION

Before we begin, let's start with how I discovered Your Cells Are Listening and radically transformed my life.

Growing up was interesting and I was always filled with a lot of self-doubt, self-criticism, felt like I could never do anything right, which led to not so nice internal conversations about and to myself. I didn't like how I looked, I didn't like how short I was, or how my eyes looked for example. Funny thing about that short part – I remember it never bothered me until someone started making fun of short people. A lot of how I viewed myself had come from what others said about/to me as well as how I perceived what they said, it shaped how I saw myself as well.

Later on in life, anxiety and fear gripped me as if I was falling down a spiral rabbit hole of illnesses, depressions, stress, confusion, and asking myself how did I end up here? I went from healthy and happy to diseased, exhausted, broken and depressed and the future looked grim.

July 20, 2016 is the day that my life truly was changed and flipped upside down in the most beautiful, authentic and strange way I didn't see coming.

There I was cooking dinner and all of a sudden, I was on my way to the floor fast. I died, right on my kitchen floor as I was preparing dinner! As I was going out, I knew I was dying. I turned to my fiancé, Sergio, and said "I'm dying" as he caught me before I landed on the floor. Now while this is happening, I was fully aware of everything going on within my body. I felt every cell, they became very active and as this rush of energy was surging through my body as I felt myself leaving my physical garment.

As I was leaving my body, I was trying to fight it, it was as if I was reaching up to pull myself back in. An attitude was coming on along with all this and I wasn't happy about leaving! Yet at the same time, the feeling was so loving, peaceful, expansive and there was a gathering of people and energy.

I was aware of Sergio in front of me and I was aware of his feelings and emotions and aware that angels were there holding him keeping him calm. I was not aware that at this point my skin had gone ash grey and my eyes were black and sunken in, and everything was dark. At the same time, I found myself in front of Jesus, St. Germain, Lord Asun, Mother Mary, Mary Magdalene, and a few others of the Great Ascended Hosts and a love of the Mothers Presence. I said "Umm...what gives, why am I leaving now?

My life is just about to begin a new, my divorce is final. I have met my twin flame and we are getting married in a few months. I am totally healed and I have a lot to look forward too, the life I have dreamed of was now coming together and I have to go? What the hell is up with that?" Yes, that is exactly what I said. I was told I have fulfilled what I came to do here on earth with my requirements in this embodiment and Jesus said he is here to take me to my freedom if I wish to still go and serve from the higher octaves OR I can go back and fulfill the covenant I made with God in 2004. Which was to help the people on earth learn the truth about life, the afterlife and unravel the hidden mysteries of the bible that man has perverted, omitted and plain out lied about to keep people in bondage and away from the truth. I was advised I would have help from all the great cosmic beings, Ascended Masters, Archangels, Avatars, Mother Father God, and the legions of angelic hosts. They downloaded into me what was to unfold. I was to share my knowledge with all those who would listen and accept the truth.

You see on this day, what I have always thought, and now knew beyond a shadow of a doubt was truth, that there is a Mother God; it only made sense to me. I have always felt that but now here I was and I knew what I was feeling was a love beyond anything I have ever experienced. I knew it was divine and it was so tender and precious. It was a different vibration from the one I was receiving from Jesus.

Ok, back to the death. I answered Jesus and the Great Cosmic Beings that were there and told them yes, I want to stay and do what I promised back in 2004. The promise or covenant I made with God back then was this...." WHEN I was healed, not if, WHEN I was healed, I would then help others to heal and experience God's love.

Why did I do this in 2004? Back then I was practically bedridden with a few mystery illnesses that the doctors could not figure out what was going on nor why. Over the next few years, the diagnoses came in of Lupus, RA, Fibromyalgia, Lyme Disease, and Chronic Fatigue. That day I made the covenant was a day that I woke up so filled with pain that it took me over an hour to get from my bed to my bathroom which is not that far of a distance. The pain in my body was so intense it took everything within me to move. I was so down and out. I did not have a support system, my husband at the time did not understand what was going on and it was hard for him to be sympathetic to me. He was convinced I was making it all up, at least that is what he would say to me. I could see the fear in his eyes and I knew, he too, was scared, but he never talked about it. Then the look of fear in his eyes changed to pity. The day I saw the pity in his eyes broke my heart in ways I didn't fully understand at the time. It sparked something inside of me that rose up and I was determined NEVER to see that look from ANYONE again. I knew I was going to be healed and nothing and no one was going to stand in my way.

Anyway, it was a very lonely time, my friends weren't calling anymore nor were they were taking my calls. I had to cancel a lot of plans as the pain and fatigue overtook me. Family stopped calling and visiting as well. No one was interested in hearing what was going on and I was called a hypochondriac. You see, I went to bed one night healthy after working out at the gym and woke up the next morning with Bell Palsy on the right side of my face and my body filled with pain I had not known before.

I didn't even understand what was going on or what was happening. All I knew was that my body was pissed off and it was revolting against itself. It was so bizarre the way it came on and how intense it was. Somewhere deep inside of me a determination welled up and as I walked back to my bed from the bathroom I stopped at the foot of my bed and said "God, I do not understand why this is happening to me, but I do know this -- from this day forward I will thank you for allowing me to experience all of this, so I can one day help others through this. I know this is NOT my truth and this did not come to stay, but it came to pass. I will mine every gold nugget I can out of this, so I can be free and help others. When I am healed, I will make it my life's mission to help others."

You see when I was presented with the chance to stay, I wanted to because I knew I had not made good on that covenant I made with God. I wanted to fulfill that so badly. Jesus told me that I was going back and the beautiful unfoldment has begun. Now it was time to do what I was called to do.

As I was coming back into my body, I must say, coming back into my body was the most jarring and uncomfortable feeling I have ever experienced. I literally felt like I was being stuffed back inside a bottle that was too small for me. As I came back in, I opened my eyes to say something to Sergio but I couldn't see anything, everything was black. I remember seeing myself in the mirror and what was looking back at me, I did not recognize. All I could manage to say was that I was very tired and needed to go lay down. He helped me up the stairs and helped me get into bed and I immediately fell asleep and received my download for Your Cells Are Listening.

I had already been practicing your cells are listening without realizing it since 2004. The download that came through was how to package this information so it would help others heal their emotional body and end the war between their mind and emotions. Your Cells Are Listening is the ancient divine answer to longevity, peace, joy, love, happiness, and abundance to bring you hope, encouragement, love, understanding and most of all answers and knowledge that you too can apply in your life right now.

This is a process to break up the destructive thought and feeling patterns that keep you from living a healthy, complete and authentic life.

I will also share with you how I came to this breakthrough realization that radically changed my life and caused a total body healing from Lupus, Fibromyalgia, Rheumatoid Arthritis, Lyme Disease, diabetes, and a 67-pound weight loss without diet or exercise. You too can have radical transformations in all areas of your life, if you choose to. I say "choose to" because it is a choice, a free will choice. It is a process and not an overnight miracle pill. We all were given free will and not even God can override that free will.

Within the pages of this book (life manual), you will be exposed to the Ascended Masters teachings that Jesus was taught in the Ancient Himalayan Mystery Schools. You will learn divine ancient truths and the Tree of Life Teachings that you have forgotten due to the "sleep" you have been under since "The Fall from Grace." I will also explain what actually took place during the fall from grace, as well as show you that you are the savior you have been looking for.

YOUR CELLS ARE LISTENING
Heal your thoughts heal your body

When you fix your emotional body, the mind automatically corrects itself. The emotional body is the feminine side of life, all emotions have will in them and will is a feminine engine that drives every quality. The emotional body is the water element, and water either gives life or takes life depending on the will behind it, or the feelings and emotions. Your feeling body is yours to get lost in.

Do you realize the power that you hold within your emotions? The mental body is masculine in nature and emotions are feminine. This is by divine design and patterns the true One Source, Infinite Father-Mother God. It is also what we have forgotten because of the fall from grace. We separated ourselves from the emotional body as it was intended to be. The masculine energy from the mind, the intellect is where creation starts, with an idea it is then designed to drop into the heart and check in with the feminine will and love side of the house to qualify the energy that is to go forth to create a substance that is essential harmlessness. THAT is what has been missing for millions of years.

Let me ask you this, do you think we would have a war if the masculine side dropped that idea into the heart? NO -- the mother energy would never qualify energy to be destructive to another life stream of any kind. Due to free will, no cosmic being, angel, Ascended Master nor Father or Mother God can interfere with that. Until you choose to turn towards the light and seek to remember.

The time is now upon us, we have entered into the Seventh Golden Age, The Age of Aquarius, the time for the Divine Feminine to arise and take its rightful place to lead the way to freedom and ascension into the 5th dimension. Not only for the people of Earth but for the planet as well. The reason you cannot see life on the other planets is that they have already ascended and are in the 5th dimension and your sight has not yet been raised to see that yet. The end of the age of man -- meaning masculinity in thought minus the feminine came on December 21, 2012. We will look back on that age as barbaric in future days as we usher in the time we have all been waiting for, hoping for, and praying for.

There is a bit of truth in all religions and all things are interrelated. With that understanding, we can start to put together the puzzle pieces to see the fuller truths. Keeping in mind that we are not finite, but infinite as is

11

Mother Father God, Source, All That Is, The Universe, The Multiverse - etc. The Mayan calendar was predicting the end of the age of man which many misinterpreted as the end of civilization. Christianity teaches about an event they call the rapture where Jesus comes from the sky and for every two people, one is taken and one is left standing. They interpreted this as the good are raised into Heaven with Jesus and the rest are left behind because of sin or not being or doing good enough. There are many, many variations to the same misunderstanding of truths that we have forgotten.

Yes, December 12, 2012 was the end of the masculine rule. The end to life as we have known it and have recycled over and over again. A new time is upon us, a divine golden age where we will see the turning back to the light and love and helping others and the planet heal from all that we have imposed out of ignorance.

First, you must start with yourself by learning how to master your own emotions and mind. True freedom cannot come to you or anything else until you do. This is not an overnight process but a day to day process that is unlike anything else you have known. Until now.

If we think of the falsehood that we all have been living for millions of years as a matrix or a hologram; something that seems so real and tangible that appears to have no escape. This is where you can start to put your puzzle together. You can think of the matrix as a video game whereby you are an avatar playing a role within different levels.

The age of man was all about living out of balance and more one-sided in the intellect and less from the heart - the love center. Think of it this way - we are two parts of one whole, yet we have been taught to stuff our emotions down and not to be ruled by emotions but by our intellect. That is what the matrix teaches, and it is backward of what the truth is.

The bible has many truths hidden within it, however, it has been adulterated and the words of Jesus edited, removed, omitted and some instances misinterpretations designed to hide the truth from the masses, especially in the new testament. This was done in 325 AD by Constantine the Roman leader who craved power and did not want the people to learn the truth of Jesus's words, instead wanted them to think that Jesus was the only one. When in truth Jesus's purpose was to be the living record of Resurrection, how we too are to follow his teachings and rise up out of the human self into our God self via the Christ Consciousness.

Another truth we have not been taught in education is that your body was

12

created to respond to the dialogue you have with yourself daily. The thoughts you think about yourself, what you say to yourself and what you believe about yourself. Your cells are your personal scribes storing every emotionally charged thought you have about yourself, and depending on what your dialogue is, life compels for all this to manifest. Self-doubt, criticism, condemnation, claiming sickness, "I'm sick", "it's flu season", etc. all must play out and come to be in your life.

The great news in all this – even if you have been very hard on yourself in the past, you have the power to change this and determine your outcome.

THE GRAND BATTLE – YOUR THOUGHTS & YOUR EMOTIONS

Do you battle a constant barrage of negative thoughts? Anxiety, depression, fear, doubt, worry, lack and a sense of hopelessness that you missed out somehow on the great thing's life has to offer?

Are you ready to stop being a victim to your thoughts and feelings? Are you ready to take your power back and heal the areas in your life that need love, light, and healing? Do you want love and are tired of getting the same old toxic energy patterns in different people? Do you want more finances and abundance in your life? Are you battling an appearance of disease and the doctors have no answers for you?

If you answered yes to any of the above questions and even thought of a few more on your own, then you have purchased the right book for you, at this time in your life. Let me be the first to congratulate you on choosing to invest in yourself and to face your biggest saboteur — YOU. Yes, beautiful heart, you are in a battle with yourself and the best way to win over an opponent is to use knowledge. Keep reading to gain the knowledge you need to take back power over your thoughts and feelings.

What if I were to tell you that you and you alone are in control of your body? That apart from you, your body can do nothing. That everything you have ever thought about yourself or said about yourself OR another person is written on the cells of your body?

Why should you listen to me about this? Well for starters, I have done it. I put what was a theory (in my mind) to the test and it has proven me right every single time. It is doing the same for my clients, both my private one on one clients as well as in my group programs and self-study courses. If one person can do it, then it is available to everyone.

Before I get started, I want to make a point that you will hear me say often and that is - no judgment. There is no room for judgment of any kind towards yourself or others. You have now entered into the "no judgment" zone, keep this in mind as you read on.

Growing up we are not taught the truth about a lot of things, but what if what we have been taught: via religion, education, parents, grandparents, teachers, friends, and society isn't the full truth? (no judgment) What if we have had it backward all these millions of years? That sure would explain a lot, wouldn't it? Keep reading, in this book you will start to get answers to your long-held questions while gaining the tools and knowledge on how to heal and change your life.

You are a vast network of thoughts, emotions, and feelings -- this is by divine design and not by accident. You were not meant to go through life clueless and trying to figure it out with reactionary responses. Not at all beautiful heart -- you were designed to know the future and to direct your life. There is no need for you to react to anything in your life. You are to know your future and you are to create and direct it with your desires. This has nothing to do with being psychic or anything like that, it is by design we are to know what is going to happen in our tomorrows.

On this journey of awakening, we are not learning new things per se, we are actually remembering truths about what we already know, but have forgotten. In this experience called life on this planet, we have covered over our divine truths: how to adapt, know, be, do, and say. We have been playing out experiences because our own thoughts and feelings are creating opportunities for such experiences to exist in our reality. We do this, because of the "fall from grace."

SETTING THE RECORD STRAIGHT – THE FALL FROM GRACE

There is a process to awakening, and there are many different spiritual paths that one can take, all of them are to be honored. It is up to each individual to decide what is perfect for them. In fuller truth, we are all here to ascend as Jesus the Christ did and help the planet to ascend. His time here on earth was a living example of awakening and ascension via the resurrection path.

To ascend, one must partake in the divine and holy marriage which is mastering your mind, emotions and physical body. Essentially you must bring them into balance as they were before the fall from grace. Buddha was a living example of this perfect and divine balance -- (the divine holy marriage). When you reach the level where you are no longer reacting and can maintain peace and harmony within yourself that no matter what the appearance you have showing up, you know the higher truth.

The core issue that is affecting the planet today is the conflict between thoughts and emotions within human consciousness. When you have thoughts and feelings that are out of balance, you have chaos.

One of the biggest fallacies perpetuated by the church that has caused magnitudes of chaos is religion's version of the beginning of the creation of life on this planet and their account of what happened in the Garden of Eden.

By definition, the word religion comes from the root word religio which is Latin and means to hold into bondage, to bind. I will leave that there and let you feel into that on your own.

The belief in two powers of good and evil (created by religion) has led humanity down a dark scary path for millions of years. Things progressively got worse in the different ages which ultimately led to the destruction of those ages and civilizations. The truth is there is only One Power, One Source and that Source is love and perfection. Anything outside of this is a creation from the belief in two powers such as a loving and punishing God. That God is a creation out of the free will of humans to control and manipulate other humans by methods of fear-based beliefs.

The truth of who we are, what we are and why we are here has been hidden from us due to our choice to separate from our Higher Self and our spiritual connection. You see, the fall from grace was not because we disobeyed God and he then punished us and we need to turn from sin and seek a savior on our behalf to go before God and say we are good enough so we can spend eternity in heaven. The fall from grace was us choosing to make things harder and experience all that life on a 3rd dimensional plane of existence offers.

We are beings of consciousness on a 3rd dimensional plane of existence on planet Earth. A 3rd dimensional plane is a plane of demonstration, a place where light beings of consciousness chose to come to experience all that we chose too in physical garments. This is not our first time here, and life does not cease to exist after we leave these bodies. In fact, death is not final in full truth, it is a transition. One where we leave our current physical garments (bodies) and return to our original state of light/energy form -- consciousness.

Not all of who we are in our true state comes into the physical body. The physical body is not able to contain all that we are, so a big part of our true self -- our Higher Self is in a higher dimension. This is your I AM presence, higher self, your true God self. It did not fall from grace, our little self, the human part of us -- that is what fell from grace.

When we all chose to come to this new planet called Earth to co-create with it and experience what is like to be god in physical forms, we passed through "veils" to protect our higher self. Awakening is the process of removing these veils.

To give a quick (as I can) synopsis of who we are, where we come from, how we got here, what went wrong, where we are now and where we are going, (since that is not what this book is focusing on per se), yet it will help give a better understanding of how we find ourselves in the Matrix; what the Matrix is and how to get out and live the life of freedom, understanding, and love we are all seeking - whether we realize it or not. It will also help to give a foundation of understanding for Your Cells Are Listening as we are all part of one consciousness on the same journey just on different paths and different levels.

Mother Father God is at the heart of creation of not only the Universe but of us and every living thing we know of creation and that is yet to be created and come into form.

Most of us are familiar with Father God -- or God as a masculine figure and have had many questions about the existence of a Mother God or the feminine in life. It took both, the masculine and the feminine - the mind and the heart - two parts coming together as one whole to create in their image and likeness perfection in the infinite universe.

You can think in terms of vibration, energy, light and they would all be accurate. You see Mother Father God, Source, All there is, God and the Holy Spirit, or whatever other names you care to call them with whom you feel comfortable. There is no right or wrong - only that is, and only God is.

In the circle of life, we are all one and one with all creation. We are here in these physical bodies having physical experiences because in fuller truth we are all both masculine and feminine and we are to bring into balance both of those polarities. Polarities like light and love, one and the same yet different parts. The masculine is the mind of God, and it is what we have been operating from for millions of years since the fall from grace. This is the light, the illumination.

The fall from grace which in fuller truth is when we shut ourselves off from the feminine, which is the heart of God, the love - the feeling side of life. Why and how did we do a stupid thing like that?

In the first two golden ages, things were so much different, we were perfection. The image and likeness of Mother Father God sent to this planet to experience what it is like to be creators in physical bodies. Now things were very different in that time because we remembered who we were and what the purpose was for being here. When we came into embodiment our physical bodies were much different than they are today. We also had an elemental being assigned to us, which when we turned from our all-knowing higher self and started killing each other, our elemental being would be killed as well. Everything always circles back to the One, infinite in nature and one with all.

God is love, light, and perfection that can only create from that which it is; therefore, anything outside of pure love (not human/duality love), light and perfection is not a "God" creation but a creation from the little self - the human self out of duality. Duality being a belief in two powers - good and evil, a loving God and a punishing God. Duality is the matrix or human version of polarity. It is counterfeit. I like to think of it as a counterfeit handbag -- museum quality -- but still a fake. Therefore, since duality is the counterfeit, the fake to the truth - anything created in and of duality will not be able to stand the test of time.

The bible is the biggest promoter of duality and it starts in the first book, Genesis. Adam and Eve are in the garden of Eden and there are two trees, one being the Tree of Life -- God's perfect tree and the second tree the Tree of Knowledge -- of good and evil. They are warned not to eat of that tree, and then a serpent came and tempted the woman who then led her husband into "sin" and that caused the fall from grace.

Wow, there is a lot going on right there first, you have TWO trees, yet the focus turns to the tree they were warned not to eat of. This is the first place we are reminded that there are TWO trees. Turn the focus off the "counterfeit tree" and place your attention back on the truth of what you have forgotten, The Tree of Life of which you are the branch, Christ is the tree and Mother Father God are the roots in which you are well grounded. THIS is the tree that grows within us -- it is us -- the flower of life blueprint.

We are not taught to remember the truths that we have forgotten because we have been in a great hypnotic sleep being force fed the "counterfeit" information from the tree of knowledge of good and evil. We are told what is truth and we must conform or believe this way or that way and it is the only way and only one can be right. This is why we have so much unrest, anger, hatred, greed, etc. running rampant through the planet. It is why all kingdoms are out of balance. Why the earth is going through the great correction, and the awakening. We are awakening to the knowledge we have always had within us that we forgot because we have been taught that duality is the right way and anything outside of that is evil and wrong and will keep you separated from God and damned for eternity. This is the bullshit programming of the Matrix, at least that is the name I gave it.

The movie The Matrix did a great job at giving us visuals to the world of duality and its programming. Think of this life that you are living right now as a hologram, a video game named the Matrix. Within the Matrix are many different programs and holograms that are all based on the same formula or equation; duality, the belief in two powers, good and evil. The Matrix cannot operate outside of this platform, the whole thing will collapse when the masses wake up and come back to their true selves and turn toward the light and serve humanity from the Tree of Life. How does one get out of the matrix? They remember how to bring into balance both the masculine and feminine energies, and live from Christ Consciousness, the I AM Presence within oneself.

There is only One Power and that power is love and that love is perfection. We are created as the individualization of that One power. Our creator who is Perfection created us as Beings of Perfection. Which means anything outside of perfection is duality. The reason this concept is hard for many to grasp is due to Perceptions. Perceptions are created in duality. Going back to the Genesis example, it was perceived that they were lacking something, which created doubt about what they already knew. Their state of being didn't change they were still perfection when they entertained the thought form of duality that they were missing something, therefore they could not be in perfection because they were lacking something.

We all came here together as beings of perfection to experience that perfection and to create from perfection in physical bodies. We were also given free will -- it is this free will to believe in two powers that makes it so. It is this free will that God cannot interfere with nor are we judged on what we chose to create. Only you have 100% power and choice over your free will. There is no being in the universe that can nor will interfere.

The goal of coming to this physical planet was to become Masters over the physical plane. You see we had never lived in a physical plane before and we all signed up for the experience to be non-physical beings in physical form, therefore bodies had to be created for us so we could practice and learn how to be Masters over energy substance and how to transmute energy. These bodies that were created for us could only contain a small amount of our non-physical energy so the majority of us in our true form Christ Consciousness remains above us in the higher dimensions of perfection.

The plan was for us to come into physicality and evolve. We were to bring more love and light within ourselves down from our Higher Self into our earthly selves until we bring all of our perfect Higher Self into our physical bodies to fully express our Individualization of Perfection. We would become our true selves on earth -- God beings, beings of Perfection expressing ourselves through these physical bodies. We would be masters of the Laws of Attraction and Manifestation, Masters over matter. Jesus the Christ is our example of doing this. He came into physical embodiment to show us how to become the Masters we were sent here to be, by our own choice.

Earth was the new planet on the block when we decided to experience being creator beings in physical bodies, aka earth suits, we referred to it as our Garden of Eden, the polarity of light and love, perfect balance of thoughts and feelings, manifesting at will whatever we conceived was how we were living. There was no waiting to manifest, it was instantaneous, whatever we desired. We were tapped in and hooked up, we had all the answers. Why is that? Our Higher Intelligence, we were one with it so any question we had instant access to all knowing. We were moving right along mastering matter and the laws of this physical universe, and got bored. We desired to understand how our polarity worked, every aspect of it.

20

We desired to understand how our thoughts and feelings worked together as energy to form matter, how that energy became things, how manifestation works.

It was here where all 10 billion of us chose to separate from our Higher Intelligence- albeit with good intentions- to become even greater Masters through trial and error instead of instant perfection. This forced us to analyze everything and this is where we started to make mistakes. We didn't have access to the perfect answers anymore. This is what is referred to as the Fall from Grace. We chose to separate ourselves from our Mind of God. At first, we thought our plan was working as we were experiencing trial and error, however as time went on, we started making more and more mistakes which led to pain -- something we never experienced before and we didn't like it so we decided to shut ourselves off from our hearts so we did not feel pain as intensely.

To recap -- we shut ourselves off from the mind of God. Then we closed access to our hearts which is the feminine side of life - the emotional body, the feminine love energy that balances the masculine mind creative energy. Our thoughts and feelings were out of balance in favor of the masculine, the mind. Without the love of the divine feminine, the Mothers Presence and without access to our Higher Intelligence to tell us that is a stupid decision with horrid consequences we became out of balance which in this state allowed our ego to become altered and take over the decision-making process. Altered ego wasted no time in jumping in and taking over. Altered ego took over because it was formed out of Ego seeing the stupid decisions we made and went into protection mode. Your altered ego is the part of you that always questions yourself, your choices your thoughts and feelings and it is where doubt comes from. It has good reason to act this way, it feels it is its job to protect your healthy balanced ego which is your true self, from your dumb choices made long ago. It perceives it is not safe -- being you is not safe.

The fall from grace was not us disobeying our creator and needing to be "good enough" to have God's favor and love, all our hearts desires, bestowed upon us so we can live the next life in heaven. Or a test that knowing what good and evil is and making the right choices all the time that is pass or fail. God is perfection, not judge mentation! We are the ones that created judgment as a way of measurement of ourselves in finding our way back to the perfection that we are, love.

21

The fall from grace is a perception that we did something so bad that we must suffer and struggle to get back in grace with our creator. The perception that we are not good enough. When in truth it is the first mistake made out of free will to want to improve upon perfection, instead of just being perfection.

At the center of our consciousness is stored the sacred geometry unique to each of us that aligns with the flower of blueprint etheric lines of the universal life force of all that is. The life force of this System of Worlds is the Divine Mother's Presence, the Divine Feminine is here to bring balance back to each of us and every kingdom on the planet and raise us into the ascension.

We were not supposed to be in this state and stuck in the 3rd dimension for 13 million years, we were to ascend and resurrect 70 years after Jesus the Christ came here to lead us back to our true authentic divine selves by showing us through his life in the physical embodiment of Yeshu Ben Joseph how to overcome the duality we find ourselves living in. He came to remind us of who we are, why we are here and how to get back.

Your Cells Are Listening is a program built on the ancient knowledge of how to bring oneself back into Divine Balance while healing and remembering how to access the information. Your Cells Are Listening (YCAL) is your roadmap out of the matrix and your fast-track plan to wholeness and freedom on the awakening journey.

Everything in the Universe is designed to work together - as above so below -- the microcosm and that macrocosm always starts with the micro. Healing and getting back to the original purpose and intent is no different and it starts at the micro level as well. This is vitally important information that needs to be understood sooner rather than later. Once you have a good handle on this, not just in your mind, but in your heart as well this journey will be a bit easier for you.

Starting at a micro level means things begin in the unseen, the micro. You are not seeing things happen on the inside at the microcellular level but they are happening all the time. Not only that you are not your body, your body is your Earth suit, it was made just for you and you have all you need to operate and control your Earth suit within you, but that is what has been forgotten and covered over for millions of years.

Allow the words on the following pages to ignite in you a deeper awakening that sparks the unfed flame in your heart and the three-fold flames of Love, Wisdom, and Power rise up and light your way to balance and freedom from the matrix and the chains you find yourself in. Let's take that step.

MANIFESTING METAMORPHOSIS

Your cells are ALWAYS listening and they are taking direction from you. No one else only you, whether you are aware of it or not, it is the truth. I ask you to stop for a moment and suspend any previous thoughts or beliefs and just think back in your life when you have said something about yourself — negative or positive — the body doesn't judge your thoughts and words it just acts on what you put out. Your body is like a giant magnet that is always on. What you are thinking and feeling sends out vibrations that will only attract the same energetic vibration of what you are putting out. Take a few moments to think back to a time where you were thinking a certain thought such as "I do not want that to happen" and then what you don't want actually happens. Of course, you are going to get what you don't want because that is where your thoughts and words are — focused on the don't. Yes, this is a universal law, The Law of Magnetism and it governs everything in our universe, but for our bodies, it is much more personal.

Growing up most of us are taught from books that are mainly filled with half-truths and misinformation formulated out of duality via theories, opinions, and beliefs. This does not give us the life instructions we need or even a solid understanding of who we are, what we are and what we are doing here, let alone truths about the nature of the Universe its laws, Earth and her plan. We have been going through life after life doing it the hard way based on faulty information. Allow me to share with you some understanding of some Universal Laws and why you need to understand how they work.

Let's take a look into what the Universal Laws of Creation and Attraction are. After all, how can one truly put these laws into action without knowing fully what they are and how to work with them, right? In order to harness the unlimited powers available to us through the Universal laws, we need to have a clear understanding of how to engage in the three forces that they respond to. The three forces are: intent, consciousness, and energy. When we develop our spiritual muscles and gain a deeper understanding of the purpose of the laws then we understand that to live the life we want and have the relationship we want, we must be aware of how we interact with the laws daily in our lives.

The Law of Manifestation shows how things come into being. In quantum physics, it is clear that consciousness creates reality. This applies to your personal life just as much. Your consciousness creates your reality. What you think on, you create.

You see, the Universal laws do not judge nor do they take sides. What do you mean, you ask? Well, the laws are always at work all the time, no exception. With that being said, the law is impartial and automatic. If you are having a thought and you say to yourself, "Well I don't want that to happen", the Universe isn't here to be your psychologist and decipher what the hell you really mean. Nope, this is not how it works. So, you see, the more you think about what you don't want, the only reason you get exactly that is because of the Law of Manifestation. It is ALWAYS, did I say ALWAYS, ALL the TIME at work, and it HAS to give you EXACTLY what you are focusing on with your consciousness, intent, and energy. So, it hands you more of what you don't want because that is what is dominating in your vibration.

The LAW OF MAGNETISM states that you can only magnetize or attract the same type of energy that you put out about yourself. Each of us projects a personal energy field, an energetic message about ourselves, which is our signature resonance and the source of much of what we attract.

The LAW OF MOMENTUM in using Sir Isaac Newton's first and second laws of motion and interpreting them from a metaphysical standpoint more so than a physics standpoint. First one, "an object in motion stays in motion unless it is compelled to change its state by an outside force, aka DOUBT, FEAR. His second law defines a force to be equal to the change in momentum with a change in time. He defines Momentum to be the mass object times its velocity. In metaphysical terms - the amount of momentum you have going in a direction is determined by the amount of emotions and thought you have, going on inside your cellular activity. The direction can be either negative or positive depending on your thoughts, emotions, and beliefs. For most of us we have been building momentum negatively and when we introduce a positive force, many times we find resistance. The resistance is there because you have more momentum going in the opposite direction of what you want.

Let me establish a foundation or background for you to build this new lifestyle around. Having access to tools will not do you any good if you do not know the proper purpose or usage for the tools.

When you do not know the purpose of an object, abuse is inevitable. If you do not know what the divine purpose of your body is and how to work with it, of course, you are going to miss use it and abuse it. No guilt or shame needs to be put on you for your past choices, we don't know what we don't know. It's what you do after you know the purpose of the object — will you continue to do the same things that have led you to the point where your body is breaking down? If so, then you are making a free will choice. This is your divine right (therefore there is no good or bad decision) and your body will continue to respond to you in ways you will not like and life will be like swimming upstream with a sandpaper bathing suit on - not very comfortable. But you hold the power within you via your divine free will to make the choice to educate yourself and get to know the purpose, plan, and design for your body.

So, you are not reading this book and taking my courses if you already know the true divine purpose of your body. So, go easy on yourself throughout this whole process as it will trigger feelings of guilt, shame, and judgment that you will need to acknowledge. Release these quickly because these are three emotions that their only purpose is to hold you captive to the old limiting beliefs and maintain your momentum negatively. When guilt, judgment, and shame appear as a stop sign, it is your body that signals to you that there is a deeper truth that wants to surface so you can see it, acknowledge it and release it.

FOUNDATION OF CHANGE

We all have an inner child. Your inner child is the foundation from where you see the world. It is also the source of anxiety, flight or fight and wanting to hide. From the time we are born we are all creating beliefs about life; Is it safe? Is it not safe? Am I lovable? Am I worthy? Am I not worthy? And so forth.

By the time we are five, our personalities are developing based on these beliefs.

To make any lasting change it is best to start at the foundation and work your way up, however, we have been taught to live life backward and to basically do band-aid jobs at fixing ourselves when we work on changing.

The foundation of you that I am referring to, is your inner child. Your inner child is that childlike innocent part of you. The part who likes to have fun, play, imagine, dream big dreams, and looks at the world with wonder and knows that you can truly be anything you want to be. This is also the part of you where deep wounds are stored, where you learned to hide from hurts, fears, anger, and traumas. The part of you that knows how to adapt, push down and hide from what is coming up for us to acknowledge and change.

As adults, we have convinced ourselves that we have successfully outgrown and left the childish part of us behind along with all the emotional issues. This is the exact lie that keeps us stuck and festering. This is why we keep pushing our "stuff" down because we feel that we have either dealt with, made peace with it or we just don't want to look at it because after all it really isn't affecting me. The problem with all of these evasive maneuvers is that you are lying to yourself and you are allowing your "stuff" to fester out of sight. At some point, it has to surface to be dealt with.

Yes, you may have made great strides in getting over different issues from childhood. However, if situations are still playing out in your adult life that are painful and uncomfortable, they trigger you and you don't want to deal with any of these issues. That tells you right there, that the root of the issues has not been acknowledged or healed. This can always be traced back to your relationship with your inner child. To start to heal the relationship with your inner child, you first need to have a better understanding of how the relationship was damaged to begin with. Damage is done that creates mistrust - distrust of ourselves, our thoughts, and choices and others. This happens through beliefs. We have beliefs about everything and we create 'filters' on how we see the world through these beliefs (beliefs = filters).

27

Many of them are disempowering beliefs that were developed as a child. Filters on how we think and believe about our bodies, jobs, spouses, other people, situations and so on. It is how we relate to the world. A belief becomes a belief by thinking thoughts over and over again and then putting feelings to those beliefs. We get back whatever we believe. Since we get back what we think and feel, the only way to change this is to change our beliefs and we can do that!

First, we have to do it on our energetic quantum level/field and then our cellular level. In other words, our consciousness along with our feeling body, mental body, and physical body. Growing up we are not taught the truth about a lot of things. Let's ponder the possibility that what we have been taught via religion, education, parents, grandparents, teachers, friends, and society isn't the full truth. What if we have had it all backward for millions of years? For example, the first 7 years of our life, the brain is in Theta state. This is important and a key to unlocking your freedom from past traumas and hurts. There is plenty of information regarding Theta state brain waves and such, but what is missing is the knowledge that the first seven years of our lives the brain is in theta state; therefore, it is in constant record mode. Essentially the first 7 years of life your brain is recording everything you saw, heard, felt, tasted or touched via all of your senses.

Depending on what you experience during these years will give you a good clue as to what is stored in your subconscious. Make this connection: by the time you were seven years old you already had formed fundamental beliefs that have been playing out in your adult life. All of the experiences whether they were pleasant or not are stored in your cells. If not dealt with properly via understanding and tools to correct or remove these stored memories the memories will show up during teenage years through adulthood as the subconscious beliefs and filters act out. They are acting out for your attention so you can be aware and make the necessary changes your body is calling and needing you to make.

What you recorded during those first seven years became your programming for how you would create your life and world. This third dimension is the plane of demonstration as it was originally designed to be. This is the plane where we came to take on human form and experience being a creator race and creating, just like Mother Father God designed it to be. This is the training realm. Think of it as practice, where nothing is held against you. Religion has mastered the skill of making people lament over their actions and choices and call it sin when in fuller truth, sin means mistake, and here in the 3rd dimension training ground NOTHING is held against you, NOTHING. Everything you have been taught about sin from the church is not true. They are mistakes, and yes you do not escape the karma of your mistakes, but mistakes are meant to learn from and move on from. You have to give yourself the forgiveness from those mistakes, without doing this you will stay stuck. We were not supposed to get stuck here for 12 million years, but here we are, stuck, thanks to the fall from grace.

To heal and change, you must look at your beliefs because those are your filters and your navigational tools on your life journey. Whether you have realized it or not, you make all your choices based on your beliefs, therefore what you experience in your reality is based on those beliefs. Only YOU can make the changes to overcome all of these. There is no magic pill to take and it will all go away, just like waiting on someone or something outside of you to come along and wave a magic wand to cure you of everything completely which is a waste of time. This is an example of another false belief that is perpetuated by religions today. If you are good enough, loved enough then God may come and grant you a miracle. Beautiful butterfly that is not the divine design. YOU are the miracle YOU have been waiting for!

We must realize and understand that to create anything, first it has to be a thought. When you put feelings into that thought it will become reality. It has too, that is the Law of Life, The Universal Law. The Universe does not judge, so what you think and feel you will create. What you feel, you make real! This is true whether you are having these thoughts and feelings about yourself or someone else. Your cells will hear it and take the instruction as if you are talking about or to them and yourself. This has been the blueprint of all of life for millions of years, and it is not going to change. So, to stop the chaos of what we have been creating and dealing with we must go to the root and change those beliefs up so we can create what we DO want.

"Your inner child is the foundation from where you see the world. It is also the source of anxiety, flight or fight and wanting to hide."

Your inner child is your mini you. It is the wounded you. You have grown up and stuffed your hurts down trying to ignore them telling yourself that you are healed or that they shouldn't really bother you. It's that part of you, you don't want to look at, the part you ignore because it feels too uncomfortable to look at it or deal with.

Your inner child wants and needs to be accepted and only you can give that to her/him. No matter who you think you need and want understanding, acceptance, and love from, the truth is you need it from you first. Until you are able to do this for yourself you will never be satisfied when it comes from somewhere or someone else.

The inner child represents your feeling side of life, the emotional body and the emotional body/feeling side of life is feminine in nature. While the mental body/mind is masculine in nature. When you fix your emotional body the mind automatically corrects itself. They were designed to work together, yet we have been at odds with our emotions and thoughts for a long time.

Healing your inner child is so vital to your healing process as it affects every area of your life. It is where many of your root filters are stored. It is from your inner child where you get the flight or fight feeling —and it boils down to a trust issue. In my practice, I have found this to be the key that unlocks the door to begin healing at the root level and it is one of the first few things I do with each and every client. The inner child is the foundation from where you perceive yourself and the world.

If you have done inner child work before, then this will be like laser surgery going straight to the roots. If you have not worked with your inner child before, then you are in for an experience.

THE PLAYERS IN YOUR LIFE

While your inner child is the "foundation" of you there are still a few more players that make up what you have known as the full you. Let us take a quick look into who they are; a small glimpse of how they show up and act in your life.

Once you start to rebuild the relationship between you and your inner child you can then start to look at the other parts of you that play major roles in your daily life that you may not have been aware of fully. Out of the experiences you have had as a child and how you learned to deal with those your shadow/ego was formed. Your shadow is that voice inside you that is critical, snide, rude, attacking, fearful, condescending, blaming, and likes to make you question yourself and abilities. It is also the place where we hide the "darker" aspects of ourselves that we do not want anyone to know about. By darker, I mean hidden, not evil. We have grown up thinking that is our voice, our true voice or our true personality. It is the part of us that appears when making choices. It's the part of us that makes us start to second guess ourselves and causes different emotions and thoughts to come up. Then we can find ourselves in a merry go round cycle of negative self-talk and self-bashing.

The inner child is where your flight or fight response is housed, and it is determined by your beliefs. Beliefs formed from the shadow side of life have roots. They are lodged in tightly and are often hidden. Since beliefs are what run our "programming," looking at how they came to be is of vital importance. Before you start to look at those beliefs, if you don't have a clearer understanding of shadow and altered ego, the other players in your life, who have been dragging you around like a caveman all your life without you even knowing, it will be a band-aid job of trying to heal. Eventually, the "band-aid" falls off and you are left with those questions again of "why does this keep happening to me?" or "nothing ever changes".

The shadow self is the negative side of your ego, your subconscious that is fear-based and negative. It is the piece of self that you refuse, deny, or repress. You know — the part of you that you stuff down. It is the part of you that you have always denied, been ashamed of, or guilty for. Fear is shadow's comfort zone and it only operates from a fear foundation. Shadow self was created from the fragmented pieces of your inner child. Shadows' creation is perception based.

As a child, you may have seen something that you were not emotionally able to comprehend and make sense of. If you did not have the support system or people in your life to help you understand these things, your inner child created coping mechanisms that essentially stuffed things down, and this became your pattern. Your inner child would have stuffed these conflicts or confusions down to bring yourself back to where you are not having those feelings of discord or uncomfortableness. It created beliefs and filters based on this information and how it coped and brought itself back to center balance. The inner child seeks balance, harmony, understanding, and love.

If you grew up with a religious structure, strict or critical parents, a portion of shadow self comes from those internal perceptions which add in another root layer to clear. Even if you had a wonderful childhood and upbringing there are still roots into your shadow self, because life is life. Meaning that we can only understand and comprehend at the emotional level we are at the time of the event. For example, let's say as a child you saw something (on tv, a movie, on the news, in your environment) that at whatever age you witnessed the event, you didn't have the emotional capacity to make proper sense of it and it created conflict and confusion. Examples include - seeing parents fight, seeing drug/alcohol abuse, tragedies or horrific news stories. These beliefs and filters are perceptions. Shadow is the opposite of your true nature, your divine self.

Shadow is different than your inner child — for your inner child, you invalidated her power and her voice, which in turn helped to create and shape your shadow self.

Shadow self - is the part of you that identifies with all the hurts, destructive thought patterns, the voices that keep you playing small. Shadow is your self-sabotage programming. Until I was able to separate this aspect of myself from my whole self and see it as a separate entity so to speak, I was not able to fully grasp its purpose and how to work with it. I could not become the person I wanted to become while denying this part of myself and refusing to look at it. There are a plethora of reasons why we do not want to look at this part of ourselves, shame, guilt, pain, embarrassment to name just a few.

Altered ego — attacks your choices and decisions. It was created after we gave up making our own choices and decisions based on our divinity and truth. It makes you think you aren't good enough, everyone else has it better. It is the talking head, the distraction creator, the fool.

The altered ego is the mind that won't stop — the constant barrage of thoughts. All you need is less than 1% of altered ego inside of you and it will continue in its insanity that it is you and you are the body. It will do whatever it takes to take you out, to keep you from knowing who you truly are, who your I AM presence really is. The more you awaken and learn the truths for your life, the harder alter ego tries to stop you. This is what you have been battling this whole time. It was NEVER God being upset with you or warning you. It was your altered ego freaking out in fear that it has lost control of the decision-making process, so it will pull out all the stops and fears to get you to knock it off and stay stuck in the box or matrix, instead of throwing away the key to the box and playing outside the lines. Altered ego perceives that it is your higher self and all-knowing and you are the body and you are to follow its voice. It turns up the volume on you because it is afraid on your awakening journey you will discover what alter ego really is and it will lose control.

You will especially experience this when you try to meditate. You know — when you want to quiet your mind so you can connect with your I AM presence and get what you need. However, all kinds of thoughts are popping up and flying at you — yeah — that is altered egos fear rising up. Altered ego knows that when you get quiet and put intention on your I AM presence (your spirit, higher self, soul, source whichever name you use or how you relate to God/Source is perfectly fine) that you are letting more of your divinity shine through and the less of a voice and control altered ego will have.

The fragmented mind perceives, the whole mind conceives.

Perception was never the natural way for humans. Perception replaced knowing. Your ego often speaks first and it always speaks fear. Your ego is outside of the authentic you. Soul is inside of you — it is the polarity to ego. You are learning to trust your higher self, your intuition, the soul inside of you, the Holy Spirit; because that is the internal voice you're hearing. The ego believes its maker may withdraw its support from it any moment, and you can, because you created ego. You created your ego without love, it does not love you. This is why you do not love you. Your ego is afraid of you!

The ego cannot truly know anything.

Human ego stores all information that comes to you through outside sources and senses. Everything you touch, taste, smell, hear or feel, the human ego stores all of that in the vast library of your consciousness which is called the human intellect. This is separate from the first 7 years of life when your brain was in the theta state. The Holy Spirit helps your earthly mind record all the incoming data from the higher realms, your I AM presence, the angelic realms, the ascended masters, from the inner world. It's all recorded in your 3 bodies - mental, emotional, and cellular.

The Holy Spirit's role is to bring it all in and store it so you can retrieve it and understand it as you need too. The more you learn to live from your inner self - your authentic self, the more light you shine from within and you grow in all areas and become closer to leaving the human intellect behind, which by design is limiting.

The goal of shutting ego up is to break as many links in the chains of constant thought. Ego is always about constant thought. Think of ego and those thoughts as a chain. Remember back in elementary school around the holidays creating the paper chains to count down the days to Christmas? Picture that or any other chain link that comes to mind — the more you can have longer gaps in-between thoughts — you break another chain in the link. The human intellect was afraid when you gave up the driver's seat of your life, so it stepped up and started making decisions for you. However, all the decisions it was making was based on all the data from the outside corrupted world. A fragmented consciousness. How did you give up the driver's seat of your life? Every time you think or speak negatively about yourself you give away your power and take your hands off the steering wheel.

TRUTH ABOUT FEAR:
FALSE EVIDENCE APPEARING REAL

FEAR - false evidence appearing real is an illusion. It is what is most effective at keeping us stuck and in habitual patterns that we programmed ourselves to believe was necessary for our good. FEAR feelings are disempowering beliefs (old thought forms/beliefs) that are designed to keep you stuck. These FEAR feelings are a part of what is called your shadow self.

The shadow self is the negative side of your ego, your subconscious that is fear-based and negative. This is shadow self's' comfort zone. It is the piece of self that you refuse, deny, or repress. You know — the part of you that you stuff down. YUP -- that sucker has a name. Shadow self was created from the fragmented pieces of your inner child. Essentially shadow self's creation is perception based. All disempowering beliefs (FEARS) are emotional wounds that are intertwined with unworthiness. We must understand why we feel unworthy. This is what I call programming. The unworthiness programming is passed down unknowingly to us by the time we are in first grade.

In first grade it officially begins, we learn right or wrong. Whether or not we are worthy. Based on how we respond to what we are learning or what is happening with the adults around us. Your worthiness and validation can only come from you — from the inner you. When you change your perception and beliefs on the inside, your outer has to fall in line and change as well. But it always starts on the inside for lasting results.

YCAL (Your Cells Are Listening) is a process that allows you to uncover what, when, where, why and who, your FEARS came to be in a gentle, loving, supportive and safe way. When you go through this process you also heal yourself from lifelong habits, thoughts, behaviors that you have asked yourself "Why am I like this? Why do I do this? Why do I react this way?"

When You Go Beyond Fear - You See Clear!

FEAR- we all deal with it in our lives and most of the time it cripples us. The more we try and move towards whatever we thought or want, the louder the FEAR becomes. Thoughts of how to overcome our fears, terrify us. FEAR is something that for millions of years has been misunderstood.

FEAR shows up daily for us in different ways and under different names.

- Anger
- Frustration
- Depression
- Complacency
- Negative thought patterns AKA Disempowering beliefs (5 human habits)
- Criticism
- Jealousy
- Envy
- Blame

These are all examples of how FEAR shows up and hides. Notice they are ALL denser forms of energy and vibration.

FEAR is false evidence appearing real, in other words, it is a filter - aka A BLOCK. A HUGE MANIFESTING BLOCK!

Everyone talks about getting over your fear & resistance and what you want is waiting for you on the other side of that fear. I want to talk to you about HOW to go beyond your FEARS and uncover why they are there in the first place so you can get past them once and for all and get on with living your dream life.

When you understand where the fear comes from and what it really is then you have the keys and tools to make the choice to go beyond the FEAR. FEAR is a filter, learned behavior or response based on various input from different sources, including our perception of mistakes. At least the FEAR that I am talking about here. I am not speaking of getting spooked or startled, or "your life is in danger" type of fear. I am speaking of the invisible FEARs that we create ourselves without realizing it. Totally different fears. These fears come at you internally in the way of thought forms. Thought forms are different than thoughts. Thought forms are thoughts that you have had long enough to develop feelings around/associated with them that they have become a belief.

CONSCIOUSNESS
TRUTH OF LIFE

Nothing can come into your experience without it first coming into your consciousness. When something enters into your consciousness and you refuse to accept any other truth and you do not waver in your truth and have no fear -- your consciousness will make it so. It has too, it is the Universal Law of Attraction.

"When you hold onto a higher truth and refuse acceptance of any other truth -- your consciousness on its own will create that reality." -Master Teacher Asun

When you have fear in any form such as doubt and worry, you repel what you are wanting to manifest. Fear is a repellant (remember the big stop sign) and it will constrict your higher consciousness (meaning it comes in closer to your physical body), then duality thinking gets involved and then acts out everything in your consciousness that you are afraid of.

This is double jeopardy. Since your energy is split, part of that energy needs to produce a situation(s) in which you can play out the fear that is in your consciousness.

In other words, if you have ANY doubt or fear around what you want, desire or need THEN your manifesting results will be less than what you want and you will more quickly manifest what you fear.

You have seen this happen in your own life without even being aware of it. The universe and all that is - do not judge or decipher your energy. It simply gives you back what is in your consciousness whether you realize it or not. It is the cosmic law and the cosmic laws CANNOT be broken. Pray and meditate to be free of ALL fear.

You will manifest more quickly what you fear -- so it must go!

To change your physical body or any situation in your life, it must be changed in your consciousness first. To be free you need to let it go in your consciousness so it no longer looks for the things you fear. Your higher consciousness was created to fulfill everything it encompasses. There is a presence that goes before you that does all things. What is that presence? Your divine consciousness -- your I AM presence. Let me explain.

What is Consciousness

Spiritual Truth: I am not inside this body; this body is inside me because I AM a Being of Consciousness.

Truth is: The Truth is that I am not in my body. I articulate myself, I express myself through this body, through its assets, faculties, and senses, yet I am not inside my body. My body is not who I am.

Allow me to expand on this. I want you to have a clear understanding or picture of consciousness: what it is, how it formed, what it does, how it works. This is vital to understanding the deeper truths of who you truly are.

I have talked about your I AM God Presence that is both above and within you, the Mother's Love Presence that is within your heart, and I have covered your human, duality ego self. With this, you have a good base for understanding, therefore, I want to go further with you. Let me explain Consciousness and how it comes to be.

When a woman is about to birth a baby, the process starts for this embodiment. When the baby's body no longer depends upon the mother's life force and the first breath is taken, what is happening spiritually and energetically, is that the first breath ignites the spark within the heart, the baby then inhales the life stream of the Mighty I AM presence. The spark lit the tiny electron in the heart and in that cosmic spark a flow of consciousness rose up through the top of the head (7th chakra) and then descended down and around the newly-formed baby body and is sealed underneath. The baby (you) body was encapsulated within the Consciousness of the God I AM that you are. Your body is WITHIN this field of consciousness, all that you are is WITHIN this field of consciousness. Your body is lovingly held within this consciousness.

This field of Consciousness is the Truth of who you are and that is why you must go a little farther each day, even if all you have is an intellectual understanding. That is fine! Show up for yourself daily, and one day you will show up and HAVE that understanding.

Let me explain it again. When you were born into the baby body and your life no longer depended upon the life force of your mother and you breathed in the spark of life into your heart electron, if nothing else happened, the physical body would fade away. And so, with the first breath when life force enters the heart and the spark touches the electron and gives it life and the life comes back through the pineal gland of the body, it fans out right and left and seals the body in a shield of Consciousness.

Now jumping ahead from birth, let me address death - what the human consciousness believes is death. Death is an illusion. There is no death. We are all eternal light beings that see no death. What we have come to know is that death is actually a transition, a change. We lose our physical garments, not our essence or who we are. When we go through the process of change called death, our Guardian Angel is there with us and the Angel reaches into the chest cavity where your electronic three signature cells are stored and removes the signature cells to take back to the plains of bliss where you await re-embodiment. Life is a cycle, and it doesn't end when you leave your physical body. You keep coming back until you have an embodiment where you awaken from the hypnotic sleep or what I like to call the Matrix. If you have not seen the 1999 movie The Matrix, I suggest you watch it with an open mind.

When you start to awaken you are put on a path that leads you on a journey to finding who you truly are and why you are here. You start to see life in a whole new way. You are awakening from the Matrix, from the illusion of what you thought was a reality, but in fact is the dream. You are awakening from lifetime after lifetime of playing in the Matrix. This is the life you have been dying to live. It is in this lifetime you chose to "wake up" from your dream state and get on with your purpose. Before you re-embody you decide what experiences you want to have to help you remember the truth. With each lifetime you have here in the physical plain known as Earth, you gain more knowledge and understanding either of the matrix or of the divine, or even a combination therein. Remember beautiful heart, there is no right and wrong, good and bad -- these only exist in the Matrix. Each of us are given free will -- it is part of the plan of the experience here on Earth. We chose to come to Earth to experience a physical planet and to create. We were given total freedom in what we choose to create. There is no judgment in that, by design. This means God does not judge what you or anyone decides to create from their free will.

Now, as I have stated before there are Universal Laws that are always at play. Let's take a look at the Law of Karma right now. The Law of Karma states that what you intentionally send out to another life stream must come back to you tenfold. What does this mean? If you intentionally send out love to another person, an animal, a plant, an element then that love you sent out to that life stream, the universe must send love with that intention back to you ten times greater than what you sent out. Same holds true if you send out negative, hurtful, vengeful, hateful thoughts, vibrations, actions the same must come back to you ten times greater. So if a human decides to use their free will to create negativity, destruction, etc. they are drawing their back to themselves with even greater intensity. God does not judge that life stream for what they are choosing to create an experience, because of free will. God doesn't come in and punish the person for doing this. It is not God's place to judge or punish-- one's own life choices bring to each what is put out. Now, it may not all happen in one lifetime. A person may need to pass through the change called death a time or two to clear that karmic debt, OR they choose to awaken and once upon the path of awakening to the truth, the karmic debt is cleared.

How can I say it is not God's place to judge or punish? Simple. Let's go back to the truth. God is LOVE. God is PERFECTION. The only god who judges and punishes is the gods of religion, it doesn't matter what religion they are, all man-made are based on duality -- the human matrix.

Once you know your consciousness is divine, and it is your soul self, your I AM presence, can reach wherever it needs to bring you the results you desire. There are no limits.

We get stuck as humans on how it's going to happen. You don't need to know HOW, you have to know WHAT'S going to happen. Well, how does that work? You co-create your reality with God and the universal forces. Therefore, you know what is going to happen. What you give your intention to, you create. You simply don't know the how -- and the how is NOT your business or job.

You are intended to always know the future. The future is what is happening in your consciousness. (Your thoughts and feelings) So if part of your consciousness entertains the possibility it might not work out part of your consciousness then has to carry a path of will that entertains that possibility.

Split energy (less than 100% focus on what you want), means the end result will be less than. So, when that experience shows up and it is not what you thought you were putting out there to manifest. you start to think things aren't working and so on. When in actuality they are working exactly as they have too. This is a universal truth.

Beautiful heart, do you now see how you truly are the co-creator of your life?

I like to use the restaurant example to give a visual to this. When you go to a restaurant you place your order, then you wait and expect the kitchen to fulfill your order just as you placed it, right? More than likely you do not watch over the kitchen staff as they go about fulfilling your order. Most likely you are out at your table with friends and talking so for that time your attention is on other things because you KNOW that the kitchen is preparing what you ordered and it is only a matter of time until your order is delivered to you. You can think of manifesting as placing your order (desire or need) with the waitress and the Universe is the kitchen. You placed your order, you KNOW that it is coming out to you. Now, for just a moment think about how the scenario would play out if you placed your order and then went to the kitchen to watch the staff prepare your meal and you are in there asking when it will be done, why is it taking so long, etc. (all the things that play out when you do not see your manifestation happen as you think it should, when you think it should). Feel that vibration out, and you can get a picture of what is going on when you are up in the mix after you place your order.

ACTION STEP: Here are a few ideas you can use to sharpen your manifesting and master this skill yourself.

- **Vision Boards**
- **Field of Dreams**
- **Get very clear on what you are choosing**
- **I AM decrees you create**
- **Vision statement**
- **Meditation on manifesting**

The more you practice shutting down the fear -- the more your consciousness is freed and the more momentum you gain as you see your manifestations start to show up in your experience closer to what you truly desire. Being aware of your thoughts, feelings and words are so important in your journey.

You will get to the point where you really get it on a cellular level that you know when life is coming at you in ways you do not prefer and that you are currently attracting this right to you. You will know to stop and immediately hold a mirror up to you and start asking "Self" questions to your cellular body.

You see we all vibrate at certain levels, and our vibration is what attracts and repels. So if things that are showing up in your experience are frustrating you --- look in the mirror and see what area in your feeling body is sending out vibrations that would match what is showing up for you. You see in "letting go" it needs to be from your consciousness, not your outer world. Meaning -- you don't let go of the desire, you let go of knowing the how. That is the miracle.

Realizing everything begins in our consciousness. What exactly is consciousness again you ask?

It is the marriage between your mental body and feeling body; both represent your consciousness. The feeling SIDE of life, the mental SIDE of life is the polar nature of your consciousness. It is to let go in your consciousness so it no longer continues to look at those things (the doubts and fears) and they stop showing up in your experience.

If you want to let something go out of your life -- weight, dis-ease, anxiety, debt, lack then you must ask yourself what is still in my consciousness around those things? You now know that you need to be 100% self-responsible in your thoughts and feelings to make the desired changes in your life. Now that you know -- you must put actions to your knowledge in order to make it a realization for your experience.

Try this - test this out -- get 100% clear on something you want -- do NOT entertain ANY doubt or fear and see what transpires. What do you have to lose in not doing this? - just the fear and doubt and I would call that a WIN WIN!! Take note of EVERYTHING that goes on. It may not seem important now, but you will see how everything is connected and how you can move through things in your life quickly by being aware of your thoughts and feelings and what changes you have made up until today.

ACTION STEP: I want you to write a love letter to yourself. You are starting a new relationship with yourself so let's make this love affair official. Write a letter, or it can be a story, whatever feels right for you. Make sure in your letter, story, poem etc. that you point out the things you like/love/adore about yourself and where you are going. The point of this exercise is to get you flowing in conscious manifesting and creating the life you want. All designers write out their plans, and you need to as well.

After you write your love letter/story then I want you to place an order with the Universal restaurant. Get detailed with your order, and then practice knowing your order is coming and not getting all into your emotions to where you are interfering with the kitchen staff working on your order.

This is where you will need to practice self-discipline. You have years of bad habits built up around manifesting and limiting beliefs. Allow this exercise to help you through shedding off all the old crap and fitting into your new way of life. Remember no judgments and have fun with this. This exercise is designed to help you see that the formula for manifesting doesn't change, it is always at work and you can manifest anything you want, once you tap into how to work with the universal laws. With all that said, some things take time.... this is where self-discipline comes in, you don't need to know the HOW or WHEN you just need to KNOW it will happen.

WHAT'S IN YOUR DNA?

Quantum is used to describe the fundamental framework for understanding how the Universe works at the smallest scales of energy. Your physical body is made up of many different parts that make up the whole. Each different system has a way of communicating with each other and with you. Your internal light body (spirit body) also has a way of communicating with your physical body via DNA. DNA is the substance of light within the physical body at the cellular level. Liquid light travels through your central nervous system via your individual DNA, communicating with every cell in your body. I won't take up your time here on the science behind this, as you can research this on your own. I do want to point out that DNA has memory and everything we think and feel is encoded into the DNA.

Our DNA when we are in high vibe and are happy allow more light to pass through hence more light travels throughout our cellular body on a whole via our light body. Likewise, when we are angry, fearful, or hurt the DNA constricts and less light is allowed through. Light and Love are the same energy and they are the most powerful forces in the universe. Our capacity to love and how much light we have in our cells are equivalent to each other. In other words - the more light you have in your cells the more capacity you have to love. Love is the key to radical transformation through self-evolvement and that begins by loving and honoring yourself.

Our minds create and our feeling body makes it real. Therefore, all that goes out from you -- must come back to you --- it is all magnetic energy --- it goes out and attracts even greater than what you sent forth.

What you feel you make real -- not just in your outer world as I mentioned, but also on your DNA and your cellular level. That is where it is all written, and gets encoded into your cellular body. We have been taught that we were stuck with our genetics and DNA cannot be altered. Yet, this is how things are passed down generation to generation because everything is encoded into your DNA and DNA is transferable. It is a light substance. Light substance is electromagnetic waves and this is how cells talk to each other. The belief that we cannot change our DNA is al false belief -- scientists around the world have proven DNA can be changed and I encourage you to do your own research.

It's when we start to make changes to our self-talk and see a different perspective in our feeling body that our cells take note as well, and encode that into our DNA and change our DNA. You see, the physical body is made up of an atomic structure aka atoms and molecules. The light body is made up of electrons. DNA is comprised in both body systems, the physical/atomic and the light body/electron. In every cell, there is a point of light, and the cells are affected by your thoughts, feelings, and words. They follow whatever you are saying and feeling. When lower thought forms such as the 5 human habits are activated by your thoughts towards yourself or another along with fear, worry, and conflict - will cause contraction/constriction within the cells, therefore, letting less light in.

There are 5 human habits that we need to remove from our lives. These five habits when we engage in them in any form, lower our vibration, they knock us so far out of the vortex - instantly - and they delay all the progress we have made. All of these are equivalent to throwing up a gigantic Costco size STOP sign into your manifestations.

The 5 human habits are:

- **Criticism**

- **Condemnation**

- **Judgment**

- **Blame**

- **Gossip**

These 5 habits stem from your altered ego. These are your red flags. These will come up towards yourself or towards another. BAM! ROADBLOCK! You aren't going anywhere and you are not going to like what is going to manifest back to you. On the other hand, positive, loving, high vibe thought forms open the cells and allow the greater light substance to flow in which in turn pushes out the dark. Think of a dark room and you walk in and turn on the light -- no more dark. The more you do this process the more light you are letting in and the more you are healing over the dark wounds. You have years of constricted, dark cells -- it is going to take a little time to bring light back into them. Each time you say your affirmations, each time you make a different choice that honors you, each time you respond from authenticity and love, the more A-HA moments on this journey of discovery, the more light you let into every cell in both body systems which in turn feed the rest of your multi-body system.

It's when we are in the lower vibrations, the human consciousness, as well as actively participating in the 5 human habits that we are constricting every cell in our body and essentially starving it to death from the light.

EVERYTHING, and I mean everything works together. You are the only one in control -- you and the I AM presence inside of you which is your direct connection to God.

We are designed to be the captain of our ship (body), your cells do not take direction or instruction from anyone outside of you-you and only you! It does not matter what others say to you, what the doctors say to you -- only what YOU say to YOU counts. To drive this point home, I will share with you how I responded to all the doctors and specialists that I had to see on a monthly and weekly basis.

The road to diagnosis is not always a straight line and for many, they can suffer for years with debilitating symptoms and not have answers or even a clue as to what is wrong with them. This was the case for me for many years, doctor after doctor, and specialist after specialist. Today there are a plethora of "chronic" diseases that doctors do not have tangible answers for. My case was a mixed bag of no answers, half answers, guesses and plenty of unknowns. The only thing that was clear-cut was the Lyme Disease and even with that being clear-cut, the standard protocol was crap. Thirty days of antibiotics and if you aren't better, they do not have answers for you, because you should be better. This led to frustration on so many levels. However, I noticed the more frustrated I was the worse I felt. I decided to not take anyone's word about my body or what was going to happen to it. This continued to grow within me and the more my body was rebelling (as I referred to it). The more pain, the more symptoms that showed up, with more trips to the doctor and referrals to specialists etc., the more questions went unanswered. Not being able to move very much gives you a lot of time to be with yourself and think, and I did not like to be idle so I started researching on my own what was happening inside of my body on a cellular level. With each medical appointment what became clear to me was this -- they call it medical practice because they do not have all the answers. Going on this idea it made sense to me that if they did not know what was wrong or how to fix me then they surely didn't know what the outcome was going to be and they only seemed to have a dim view of my future. I did not like the lens they were looking through. The more I was told I would not get better and the best I could do is manage my symptoms and hope for the best caused an Ah-ha moment for me.

I realized that they were not going to have the final say over my health and life. After all, I saw these people for a maximum of thirty minutes at a time via an appointment. They had no clue what I have been through in life, what makes me who I am etc. This was a turning point for me and from that moment forward it didn't matter who it was -- I spoke my truth and I let them know it every time they told me I would not get better I said, "That is NOT my truth, one day I WILL be healed."

Sure, they called me crazy and out of touch with reality and I had more than one doctor refer me to a psychologist because I refused to accept reality. I would stand my ground and respond with "It may not be your reality that I will get better, but it is MY reality and one day I will be healed, you will need to apologize to me for trying to put your doubt on me. I know I frustrated the hell out of them but I didn't really care, after all, it was my life, not theirs and I was not about to trust it to people who really had no interest in the outcome.

In 2004 at a well-respected teaching University Hospital with the head of chronic disease at the assistance of a family member, I thought I would find a glimmer of hope. I go hoping to get the care and understanding that I so desperately was seeking at that time. Fibromyalgia was not believed to be a real thing back then and due to my age at the time, doctors were not taking me seriously saying I am too young for anything like this to happen to me so obviously I must be depressed and seeking attention.

This was a sore spot for me. After all, I was a scared 33-year-old in a new marriage, with a new baby, and a 10-year-old at home. I found myself overnight fighting a battle I had no idea about and no real support on the home front. My husband at the time didn't believe the situation and stated I wanted attention. My parents did not want to believe me nor really hear about the problem, my best friend wouldn't believe it either. While a part of me understood -- hell I was having a hard time believing it myself - but I could not deny my body no longer was working in the basic ways I needed it to function and the pain was unlike anything I had experienced before. I get to the appointment and the doctor walks in, he takes one look at me and asks what could be wrong since I look so healthy and I am so young. Defenses up! This had not started out as I had hoped, but more as I knew it would go -- more of the same from the medical community when they are faced with new crap and it is flying in the face of their "practice" and scientific theory.

I explain what has happened and what I have experienced while my then husband sat with this scowl on his face and shaking his head. The doctor asks me to get off the table and walk to the door and back so I do, and when I sit back down, he looks to my ex and then back at me and says "There is nothing wrong with you, your gait is fine, your too young to have anything of the symptoms you say you have."

That was it -- I was NOT going to sit back and just take this bullshit -- no way. Before I know it out of my mouth flies "What the fuck do you know? After all, you are just practicing, you have spent all of 5 minutes with me and had me walk to the door and back." My ex and another family member were floored and livid and they start in on me for talking to a well-respected colleague and he knows what he is talking about and whatever he says is the truth. At this time the doctor who just finished belittling me and my symptoms says he doesn't think anything is wrong with me, but he is starting a groundbreaking study on CFS - Chronic Fatigue Syndrome and I would be a perfect candidate for that study.

So right there in the office with the doctor and these two all trying to tell me I am making things up and on and on, I came unglued in the most interesting way. Righteous anger was rising up within me like I have never experienced before and I was not about to listen to the bullshit. I will spare you all the details, but basically, when I stood up for myself, I was offered a visit to the psychologist because obviously, something was off with me especially if I am discounting what the specialist says. Here is how my response went, "Wait, what? You just said there is nothing wrong with me and I am faking all this for attention, yet you think I am a perfect candidate for a groundbreaking study you are heading -- I see what is happening here, this is all about you and your practice and name and not about me or helping to find out what is going on with me. Fuck you and your study I will not allow you to practice on me especially since you think nothing is wrong with me."

I wish I could tell you this was the only encounter like this I experienced, but it was not, it was the norm. This sent me on a path to find my own ways to help myself and I did a lot of research. It took another 3 years before I would get my first diagnosis confirming what I had been saying all along - Fibromyalgia. Then after the first diagnosis came in, the rest started showing up. In 2008 I was diagnosed with RA, in 2010 when I was at Duke University Hospital the Lupus diagnosis came in. The more medication they piled on to help with whatever new symptoms, more diagnoses came. Not to mention the addition of a chemo drug for the Lupus, yup fun times.

This drive and determination came from somewhere way deep within me and I had no idea what I was doing -- there was an inner force driving me and I was so desperate I would have tried anything. Funny thing was, as soon as I started talking to my body and listening to what was happening within my body when I did, I knew I was on to something. I was receiving immediate feedback!

For example, when I would tell my body that it didn't hurt, and it was going to be a good day and we were going to move around. With each movement I was getting closer to my healing -- and my body responded.

Now that I had a diagnosis, I had something with a name I could speak directly too. I realized that these disorders were, in fact, energetic entities, essentially stuffed down emotions and negative thoughts and feelings I had about myself. I started speaking to my body -- telling my body that this was not our truth and all of this came to pass and there was a great discovery underneath what I was going through and I was determined to find it.

This also helped me to further test my theory that my cells were listening to everything I felt and thought internally. This also helped to ignite a fire of determination from deep within my consciousness. It was awakening and it would not be silenced any longer. I was not going to be a victim to this or anything else.

I did not fully understand what was taking place within my body or what was going on, all I knew was one night I went to bed fine and the next morning I woke up not fine and very different. After much internal dialogue around this, I finally said, "No... this is not my truth. There is a much bigger picture here and I will get to the bottom of this. I am NOT going out like this." I said to God - "God -- I may not understand what is happening but I do know this -- I know this came to pass, it is not here to stay and I will not build a Hilton in my misery, I will push through and I will be healed, and when I am, I will help others get their healing too. There are valuable keys for me to find in this situation and I will find them. I know you did not "give" this to me as punishment or anything like what the church is telling me. This came on way to fast and strange and it does not belong to me. I thank you for this opportunity to grow and learn and overcome this. Today is the first day of my gratitude for all these symptoms, and each day I will thank you for all that I will experience as a result of this, because I know without this, I would not have the experience and knowledge to overcome the appearances in my life that keep me from living a victorious life."

Now don't get me wrong here, just because I accepted this and chose to be in gratitude does not mean the load got lighter, not at all and far from it. It was more like the heat got turned up on high and I had to now walk my talk. This provided many situations to speak my truth and stand on my truth. My truth was just that, my truth. It wasn't anyone else's and I was ok with that, but I knew I had to stand my ground and not waiver and not let the opinions of others sway me. This is crucial to overcoming all appearances in your life, no matter what they are, illness, financial, family, etc.

With all these diagnoses came a lot of prescription medications just to help me get through the day and slightly manage my conditions. All of the different prescriptions which were similar to each other created their own set of issues which creates a bigger hole one must decide to climb out of. The different compounded chemicals in these drugs react on different receptors in the brain, with some shutting down pain receptors and others rerouting the synopsis. Some crossed the blood-brain barrier while others did not. During this time, not one medical specialist brought up natural holistic ways to help -- and they are out there. All of this taught me that in our society we are taught to run to the medical professionals for everything and to trust what they say and not question things. I found myself thrown into an area I was not equipped to handle but quickly learned I had to be my own advocate and if I wanted to get better, I needed to do my own research and listen to my body.

It was through this I realized that these disorders were, in fact, energetic entities, essentially stuffed down emotions and negative thoughts and feelings I had about myself. I started speaking to my body more directly -- telling my body that this was not our truth and all of this came to pass and there was a great discovery underneath what I was going through and I was determined to find it. I put into practice self-love, and it wasn't comfortable at first, but I stuck with it and eventually, I saw the changes.

I want to encourage you to be your own advocate and do your own research. Talk to your cells and be guided by your intuition. Your intuition comes from your heart and it is never wrong. Where we trip up is when we listen to our mind which is usually ego based if those thoughts have not been dropped down into our hearts. You are your best advocate, you know your body better than anyone -- no matter what others tell you. The road is not easy -- but it is doable, you can stay the course while holding onto your truth and learn to hang on when the storms come to knock you off course.

One of the biggest things you will need to face head-on and continuously be aware of is doubt. Doubt will come up every chance it gets, especially when you start this work and start telling yourself how beautiful you are, how healthy you are, how wealthy you are when you have appearances acting up in your life. Doubt will tell you all kinds of things to get you to knock it off. It can feel weird at first like you are lying, but stick with it, push through the resistance, your freedom is on the other side of resistance.

What I am saying is do not impede your progress with doubt! Doubt is an instant stop sign to anything you want to manifest or create. You have lived with doubt for way too long, there is no room for it in your future. The sooner you start to shut doubt down the sooner your micro will be your macro and you will have evidence that what you are doing is working.

To see the results that you want, you have to dig down deep and stir up that determination inside you. No one, no master, no god, no angel or cosmic being will do it for you. You will learn what the Law of Continuity and the Law of Momentum are all about. Knowing, Consistency and Determination are your keys on this journey. There will be days that are amazing and days that suck -- it is how you choose to deal with the energy as to how you will come through it. You are striving for balance in both mind and emotions, this is something you haven't done in millions of years, go easy on yourself - this is the hardest journey one faces, and it is the journey inside to face yourself.

THE BEAUTIFUL MIND- THE MENTAL BODY

The universe is polarity; therefore, everything is polarity. Polarity is magnetic and electric forces coming together. The physics definition of polarity is mutual opposition, a relationship between two opposite attributes or tendencies. The mind has been referred to as the mortal mind, monkey mind, carnal mind, sinful mind, the list goes on. These words I still use and are accurate, they are just not complete in explanation of which mind these refer to or speak of. You see, beautiful heart, another perspective has not been fully explored and taught.

There is a polarity to the mortal mind.

You may have heard of dual-minded and this term is thrown around in religions around the world today. Or that the battlefield is in the mind; our sinful human nature wants to keep us away from the mind of Christ and one must die to that mind or forever be kept away from God. (There are many different versions of this story or what the bible refers to as a truth). In truth, that is a version or a partial truth. However, it is not the whole or fully accurate view. Religion teaches that this is a bad, shameful thing and it will keep you from ever knowing the love of God and being accepted. (This is the illusion designed to keep you in fear and away from the fullness and light of all that God is.) God is love, period. There is no duality in God, this is only true of the man-made God that religions worship.

Mind is a beautiful place, precious heart. Everything is created in the mind of God. Sit with that just a moment and feel that sink in. The mental body -- everything that is - was first created with a thought. Yes, the mind is where EVERYTHING is first created. It is the garden of creation - **your** garden of creation. It is the masculine polarity of God. That is your mind by divine design. Yes, the mind is the masculine energy.

Now, when you do not know the purpose of something, abuse is inevitable. Meaning, everything has to have a creator. We can think of this in terms of a product. Let's think of a laptop. The manufacturer is the creator and the laptop is the creation or the product. The laptop comes with instructions of some kind that guides us on the proper way to operate it and treat it if issues arise. It is always advised to learn as much as you can about your product so you can work with it efficiently, effectively, safely and get the most out of it for the longest time possible.

Now, how many of us really fully do that? We get a little bit of working knowledge or we learn from others some tips and tricks, but we do not immerse ourselves in ALL that it can do (well maybe you do, but I am one that doesn't for the most part unless it is something that I am so passionate about I can't sleep), and once we have what we feel is enough we are off and running. There is nothing wrong with this per se. Yet, if we keep running like this, eventually we are going to run into issues and then be at a loss for what to do. The truth is, the answers could have been found or the issues could have been avoided completely if we fully understood the purpose of this product and how to work within its purpose. Without this knowledge abuse is inevitable.

Abuse as a noun by definition is an improper use of something. So the improper use of our words, thoughts, feelings, deeds and so on is an abuse of our minds, bodies, and spirit. The truth or a fuller perspective of the carnal, mortal mind is that we have not understood fully the true purpose of our mind so we have been abusing ourselves.

The polarity to our duality mind (the belief in two powers, good and evil) is our spiritual mind - our God mind. This, in the fullest truth, is our Christ mind, our Christ consciousness. There are many different names that it is called and there is no right or wrong when it comes to what you refer to it as. You may refer to it as your higher self, your spirit self, etc. Use whatever name resonates with you, and allow yourself the permission to change the name if it no longer resonates. I call it my I AM presence, my higher intelligence, my higher discerning self.

This part of our mind is our divine mind; the part of our mind that is in contact with God and the higher dimensions. This is the "peace of mind" we love to have and experience. This is sacred divine all-knowing space and it is real. It is your authentic self and makes up part of your fourth body which we will get into later. For now, know it as your divine mind.

Right now, your mind is still a wild stallion that needs to be tamed. With dedication, determination, consistency and allowing yourself to recognize when shadow and altered ego are on stage acting out, you will be able to shift into a different space. Each time you do this, you are taking control back and rewriting your belief system and gaining MOMENTUM!

The minds mastery is found in the heart

YOUR SMART BODY

What is innate and what does it mean? Why is it important to know this? Innate by definition means existing from birth. natural, inbred, native, intuitive. Understanding what innate really is for you is a key to radical manifestation. Notice I did not say rapid manifestation. I said radical and radical comes AFTER the process and the process is the discovery, it's the journey. We are making miracles happen every day.

You know your innate body as your DNA. I briefly introduced you to your DNA and what it is in the previous chapter. Now, I will expand a bit on this because it is really in your divine smart body where your thoughts, feelings, and emotions are stored. From this point on I will refer to the cellular body with these different terms that are interchangeable -- cellular, innate, DNA, and smart body system.

Your innate body -- it is a mystery, well why is that? It is not a brain function. It is not a body system that is centralized. Meaning it is not ruled by brain function. This is not proven yet -- but it is seen often. It will be proven soon. It is often seen in hospitals, and medical science can't fully explain it. Innate is DNA. DNA molecules are always in communication with each other. Ever wondered how your body knows which kind of cell it needs and where it needs it? Innate.

Literally from birth, remember the definition of innate is "given at birth". DNA is the esoteric central command center. It is the field around trillions of DNA that knows itself as one entity. Innate. There is no one singular part of one organ responsible for innate, like brain function as being a central command. Every single part of the body is involved in the smart body system - Innate. So I said that science has not fully discovered this yet, but it is out there in different forms like muscle testing, kinesiology, and taping. Which all give you smart feedback to find out what the smart body wants to tell you. These are all outward functions to your physical body to get the smart feedback from your inner body.

YCAL is another form of this, however, it is the INWARD way of getting this information. By going at it from the inside and understanding you are a unique individual. The way to change your life and create miracles that are perfect for you is to get to know you, the authentic you and develop the best relationship you have ever had with you. This is how lasting change takes place. You are on the journey of reprogramming your life. Taking your power back that you have been giving away to others and not being fully aware of it. You are learning to control your emotional body and take charge and have a direction for your life.

With muscle testing, kinesiology, taping and YCAL you are talking to the innate field (smart body) -- your cellular body, your DNA, and you are not just speaking to ONE specific organ or gland and this communication is NOT coming from the brain. Medical science has seen this but they do not understand it. They don't understand it because it is Quantum and they have been looking at it from the 3d level. However, it is coming and this will be known. It is body-wide all at the same time. Anything that has DNA in it is innate. Innate is everywhere where DNA exists in any form and it is totally unique to you!! That is why precious hearts, this journey is so unique and you can feel alone at times. It truly is a one on one unique journey, yet the process of talking to your cells and taking control of your life is the same, the outcome and journey are unique to each one of us.

You must Love Yourself

Almost all of our blocks can be traced back into our childhood. Even if you had a great childhood and no major trauma there, I am going to show you the hidden ones that are keeping you stuck! Think back to your 2 - 3-year-old self and if you are having a hard time seeing that exactly just try to focus in on a child of that age. Now picture yourself about to put your hand on a hot stove. What do you think you are thinking at that moment? What do you think you are feeling? Now, here comes an adult — mom, dad, grandma, babysitter, brother, sister and sees what you are about to do. "STOP! DON'T TOUCH THAT!" Whoa—-feel the difference in how you are feeling about what you are about to do and how this adult is making you feel about it. At that age, you did not have the emotional ability to interpret that for what it was — someone reacting out of fear (fear of you getting hurt) they screamed at you or hit your hand away. You internalized that and had a feeling and thinking the reaction to that which was stored in your body at a cellular level. It said something like this - "You're stupid. Your bad. You're wrong. That's scary. You are not worthy. You are not loveable. You can't' do anything right." You see where I am going with this, right?

After that initial shock to your happy innocent system, the adult after seeing you are ok and most likely crying now either hold you and scold you or just yell at you. Either way, the message you are receiving is the same — you were wrong, you were bad, somehow you should have known better. So, you accepted that because no other perception was ever presented to you.

You didn't have the emotional capacity to recognize the reaction of that adult for what it really was. A reaction out of fear and guilt rising up within themselves. Fear you will get hurt and guilt because they didn't protect you enough or keep a better eye on you. It had nothing to do with who you are authentically, or how lovable you are, worthy you are, how smart you are. Things that we tell ourselves we are not because that is how we perceive what others are telling us or feeling about us.

Ok, so you have had a lifetime of experiences since that two-year-old self. The experiences with those types of reactions over all these years, added with the validation of the belief you accepted about yourself from others based on your emotional maturity at the age of when it happened. The key point (goal): to love yourself first. Why? You cannot fully love another until you fully love and accept yourself. You must love being alone with yourself. This doesn't mean you still can't yearn for partnership. It does mean that you must make peace with where you are right now. Enjoy this time getting to know yourself and living daily in the feeling of knowing you are worthy and there is that special person looking for you at the same time. You have to release your thoughts of time (when, how, where and who). These are NOT for you to try to figure out. Let it all go. Until you are 100% comfortable with being yourself and enjoying your own company - you are not ready to share your time with a partner. I hear you saying, "But I am there, I am just tired of being alone and wish to have someone to share things with." "I have been waiting and I do like my own company I am just tired/bored of it." "I do like myself, I have worked hard to get to this point." While these seem like valid reasons --- let's be honest, EXCUSES -- to not fully accept responsibility for your own happiness. After all, it isn't your fault. This is what we were taught as humans growing up.

 Why is this the most important step that you HAVE to accept and do before you can manifest the radical transformations and relationships? You are still subconsciously expecting another person to make you feel loved and worthy. THAT is your old pattern and you must eradicate it otherwise you will keep repeating it.

"You cannot change what you will not confront"

YOU ARE THE ONLY APPROVAL YOU NEED

We are constantly looking for acceptance and approval -- outside of us. As humans, we spend our lives living from an outside perspective. What does this mean exactly? We say "if so and so (they) said/did this - i.e.: call, tell me what I want to hear; etc. (feel free to fill this area in with your 'expectations") THEN I will feel loved, happy, complete, _____ (fill in the blank with how you would feel if they did what you expected/wanted).

WHY?

It's what we were taught while growing up, without even knowing it -- it is written in our subconscious. We must recognize it, cut it off at the roots and replace it with our new truths. Growing up we are taught to do behaviors that seek approval from others. If we behave in certain ways we get rewarded. Instead of reinforcing that we are loveable and ok just as we are, it is only reinforced if we behave in certain ways around different people. AND... it is ALWAYS changing based on the people you are around.

For example, did your parents show you love and reward you in certain ways just for being you? Or was it behaviorally based? What about your grandparents? Your teachers? This is by nature a faulty system because it is based on other people's thoughts, emotions, and actions -- which are always changing. As adults, we are learning a different way to get back to what God designed. In trying to get there we have to rewrite or unlearn all that we have learned. On this journey -- we are learning to love ourselves the way we were intended to love (unconditionally) and having others' approval is not necessary.

THE EMOTIONAL / FEELING BODY -- THE FEMININE SIDE OF LIFE

The emotional body is highly important to us on this journey. It is from the emotional/feeling body that we experience life. Our minds create thought, our emotional bodies manifest the experience. Your feelings are the gas pedal in your manifesting vehicle, and your thoughts are the steering wheel. You know how the mechanics of driving a car work, you can have your hands on the wheel (thoughts) but if your foot isn't on the gas pedal (feelings) pushing it down you are not going to go anywhere. There is a formula to manifesting the life you want, and the larger side of that equation is the feeling side of life. Your feelings have vibration behind them, and this is how you communicate to the universe. Think of yourself as a vibration magnet, you are going to attract back to you what you are vibrating out. Your emotions are stored on your cellular level, how you feel is played out in your body. Emotions are king and they are key to what you experience in your daily life. Your emotions drive your day, because what you feel you make real.

Do you ever feel like you are a raw nerve and everything is rubbing you the wrong way? This is one example of when your emotional body is out of balance relating to limiting beliefs. When you master your emotions you master your life, and when you master your life there is no stopping you. The sky's the limit and everyone in your sphere is touched because of it. Emotions are powerful and they are the larger part of the equation for manifesting, so learning how to master your emotions is just as vital as mastering your thoughts. Your Cells Are Listening is a program that will help you master both your thoughts and emotions and put you back in the driver seat of your life instead of a passenger in the back seat.

Remember, a belief is only a thought that you kept thinking until it becomes a truth to you.

You catch feelings from your thoughts. When you "catch" feelings or shall I say more properly when you develop feelings from your thought forms, this is what you will manifest.

This inner journey of self-discovery and awakening will have you examine all of your beliefs; this is an amazing thing. It's not the most comfortable at times, but in the end, you realize it is what you have been looking for the whole time. The power to heal yourself has been inside of you the whole time. Now you have enough human experiences and beliefs behind you that you can now allow the *knowing* inside of you to come forth.

The cells in the human body regenerate daily and the only person they get their instructions from is you. When that clicked for me, I was like hey now -- wait a minute, if my cells regenerate daily AND they only listen to me, then I am the miracle I am waiting for. So thus, began my journey into Your Cells Are Listening. I immediately went to work and tested this out on myself. Every time one of my doctors would tell me again the statistics of whichever disease, we were discussing that day I would say, "That is not my truth. I understand what you are saying, but I am telling you, that is NOT MY truth. One day I will prove it to you." The times that I did that my body instantly responded, I felt it. I felt different. I compared how my body felt when I accepted what I was told as my truth and boy was there a difference.

I also did this on a daily basis and tested it out for myself and I highly encourage you to do it as well. Watch how your body reacts and feels when you speak negatively or when you qualify that you do not feel well, then the next day do the same thing but with positive qualifications, i.e. - Today I am feeling better than yesterday, Today I am filled with gratitude, Today I am one day closer to my healing -- or whatever it is for you, just make sure it is positive.

THE PERFECT STORM
MATRIX EMOTIONS THAT KEEP YOU STUCK

Doubt, fear, anger, depression, negativity. Judgment, criticism, blame, gossip, hate...etc. Are all lower forms of energy but just because they are lower does not mean they are not powerful! Think of lower as dense, heavier -- weighing down. Just like a CAT 3 hurricane is still dangerous it is a lower form of the higher energy vibration of a CAT 5 storm. Don't get stuck on just the physical hurricane, I am using this example metaphorically for your inner world as well as your spiritual landscape. Why do the lower, dense energy vibrations seem to pack a punch when you feel or experience them? For starters, they have had millions of years of human energy of the same form attached to them -- in other words, they have A LOT of momentum built up behind them. The second reason is our mis-qualification of these energies. All too often we justify the emotion, therefore, making them true to us, instead of seeing them as an opportunity to look at a different perspective and make a different choice.

They are all designed out of duality and based on the knowledge of good and evil. They are not God qualities - they are man-made god qualities (the god of religion). The reason they feel the way they do when you experience them is due to the fact that the emotion is an offense to your authentic nature, the God in you. They are letting you know that there is a deeper truth that you have yet to realize, and upon realizing the truth the emotion goes away. You hit the illusion with the truth and the illusion must disappear. All lower vibrations when hit with truth must transmute.

WHAT YOU FEEL YOU MAKE REAL!

When you allow doubt, fear, anger, or lower vibration emotions into your feeling side of life you are telling the universe to give that back to you in your experience and at some point, it MUST be balanced. All of what you think, feel and say are written and stored onto your cellular level ...your DNA. It is the same for the planet. Every negative thought form, anger, depression, hate, and so on, it is stored on Gaia's DNA, it's the cellular level and it has been stored for millions of years. Just like in our physical garments (our bodies) over time it starts to break down and all kinds of things start acting up like never before.

We can see this playing out on the Earth right now with what is going on with the planet at this time. It is time for balancing of the energy as we

61

move forward with the 7th Golden Age and awakening. We are being called to balance the dark and light side of our being just as the earth is calling to balance herself from all the things humanity has done against her. Just like Gaia, your body is doing the same thing, your body is calling for balance and the only one who can balance your body is you.

How do you bring your body back into balance? You start from the inside -- a divine truth is this *look after your inner activity, and the outer will reflect the same.* This is what Your Cells Are Listening (YCAL) shows you how to do. It is your roadmap to this inner journey called awakening and how to heal your life.

MISTAKES ARE OPPORTUNITIES

What we have always called mistakes are actually valuable lessons we needed to learn so we can reprogram our limiting beliefs. What we were conditioned from birth onward is to be afraid to make a mistake. The lessons we learn from "mistakes" touch us on multiple levels. Picture an onion, it is one item yet when you peel off the skin you see layers. I now refer to "mistakes" as diamond fields. There are many faucets to a diamond, just like mistakes but every faucet holds a key to growth expansion.

Until we learn to change our perspective on the way we have always seen things in life, and encode new beliefs we repel what we need, out of FEAR of repeating the same patterns.

A Law of Life is this (Universal Law -- law of attraction) What you feel you make real. So, if you are feeling any of those denser vibrational emotions then you are going to attract more experiences to you of those same vibrations. The Law of Attraction, being a universal law doesn't judge what you put out, it responds to the emotional vibration you are putting out via your feelings. You see the key to the Law of Attraction is your feelings, your emotional side of life. In other words what you think about is only a portion of the formula. When you put emotions behind your thoughts ...BAM, now you are activating the law of attraction. This works for both the positive and the negative.

The easiest way to attract all the 'bad' things and the things that limit you is by worrying. Worry is a fear vibration in your feeling side of life and anything you vibrate in your feeling body works through the Law of Attraction and must attract to you more of the same. Let's face ourselves and know the truth:

"If I internalize worry or anxiety about the issues and challenges in my life, I will draw to me more of the same. 'What I feel, I make real.' If I feel anxious, if I feel the struggle, I will draw that to me."

Control: We all have the desire to control our environment. This was God's design; however, the world consciousness has twisted the true intent of control. We are not ever to control other people. We are to control ourselves, our way of thinking, to control what happens to us by what we think, say and feel. We are co-creators with God over our lives.

What routine patterns are keeping you stuck?

Your patterns and routines have energy and vibration to them. If you keep doing things the exact same way every day, you should know exactly what is going to play out in your tomorrow. More of the same, it has too because the universe responds to energy and vibration and your disempowering beliefs and patterns are filled with that energy so that is what you will get back.

What you need to do is interrupt those energy signal broadcasts. You need to change the vibration. To do that you need to break up your patterns.

What patterns am I referring to?

- Do you have a set time you wake up every morning?
- Do you have the same breakfast and coffee every morning?
- Do you drive a certain way to go to the store?
- Do you have favorite stores you always shop at?

Are you starting to see where I am going with this? What to you may be comfortable and "the routine" and how you like to do things, to the Universe it is the same old vibration. Predictable, safe and automatic. Automatic in this case means HABIT!

Since birth, we have learned that it is comforting to have a routine and it is safe and this way you know what to expect, so you can minimize the unexpected surprises. Did you notice how you just read that you automatically went to negative surprises? Positive surprises didn't even cross your mind. BAM! That's my point.

That is a habitual way of thinking and it can be changed! It is only a habit after all. We were conditioned to think this way and it has been going on for millions of years. It is an energy pattern that carries a vibration.

Let me prove it.
You have heard of Murphy's Law, right? Everything that can go wrong, will go wrong. This is a theory, an adage that carries its own vibration. When someone buys into this theory or says "Well that's Murphy's Law" they are believing in it, giving it their energy and calling that forth into their experience. This keeps the cycle and pattern going. I call this stinking-thinking. It is BASED in NEGATIVITY! So if you are saying affirmations and doing all that you can to learn about the law of attraction and how to manifest yet you subscribe to the Murphy's Law theory (even just joking

around) (and remember your cells do not know the difference) you are out of habit sending mixed energy and the old habitual one which has much more momentum (from experience...remember it's a habit) is the one that attracts the most. You will get little breakthroughs or manifestations here and there because the law of attraction does not judge your energy, it will match it.

To break up with your habits, you need to make different choices and be consistent until that becomes your new default, your new habit. You can start today by doing something as little as changing the way you drive home, or wake up a little bit earlier and spend "me" time whatever and, however, that looks like for you. For me it would be sitting in the quiet of the morning meditating or saying my decrees, getting to spend the extra time doing my spiritual practices. For me, early morning is the best time where I enjoy meditation the most. Another example would be stopping to get a Starbucks instead of making my coffee at home. You choose what "me" time looks like for you, as long as it is not the same thing you have always done. Start making different choices where you have routines or patterns that could have old disempowering energy associated with them somewhere in the history whether you realize it or not.

For example, if you have gone through something traumatic on any level, say a divorce, a breakup, a sudden unplanned change and you created routines or patterns to feel safe, secure and comfortable, you are still doing the same things today and that old energy is still there. You don't have to make drastic changes if that does not feel right for you. But if it does resonate with you and you have been feeling that urge to make bigger changes know that it is safe and appropriate to do so IF you want different results.

YOUR ACTION STEPS TO CREATE A BREAK IN THE CHAINS: Write down your daily routines and see where you can start making small changes to break up the vibration.

CHAKRAS - YOUR DIVINE GPS

CHAKRAS AND YOUR MULTI-BODY SYSTEM

Understanding not only what the chakras mean, but how to work with them in relation to the sacred practice of talking to your cells for healing and transformation is a powerful tool. Chakras relate to our beliefs, fears, needs, and desires as human consciousness and divine consciousness. I refer to it as our Divine Guidance System, and when we understand this beautiful system, we are able to radically transform our lives and heal in so many ways.

Chakra means circle in motion (spinning wheel) in Sanskrit. How I think of them - Circles of Life. Chakras are energy centers where the prana moves through. This prana is substance you can actually see, this is life force energy. Have you seen white tiny shining/shimmering particles floating in the air? That is prana!

Chakras spin with the life force energy we take in when we go into meditation connecting with our I AM presence, or they can close up (constrict) when we are more in our human consciousness mortal mind, monkey mind.

This is how we get out of balance in our multi-body system.

Deep breathing in meditation is so important as it literally brings in the prana your cells are craving and it has a calming effect on your body. You are literally taking in life force energy from the source. We have been taught to view life as linear, from A to B, in a straight line. When life is really circular. Within that circle is the oneness with Mother Father God and all that is, how everything affects another and how the butterfly effect works. It is the One Consciousness, the Christ Consciousness.

There are 7 main Chakras that I will address in this section. There are many more chakras as they are infinite and evolving but that is for a later time. This is only an introduction and foundation into this divine energy guidance system and how we are to work with it to navigate life. The Chakras are so much more than what I write here and when we have a greater understanding of them, we can go into the deeper aspects, such as how our Chakras relate and interact with our planet. When we fell from grace we moved from our higher chakras – heart and above to our lower sacral chakra and that is where humanity has stayed. Now with the Great Awakening. Happening the way has opened up for us to move back into our upper chakras and live life from the heart.

Each chakra has its own color and relates to certain areas in the body as well as functions and senses in our multibody system. You can think of the chakra system as your divine innate guidance system in action in your human physical garment. You know you are not your physical garment -- that is just on loan to you while you have this experience here on earth, but you forgot how to operate and drive your system. Your true authentic self is your divine I AM presence self. So, it is your D-GPS (divine guidance positioning system) that takes in the prana sends it through the body where it needs to go.

Think of a Hollywood movie where beings are in human bodies and they have an internal energy system that they can tap into and get help, in controlling their physical garments. There is truth in that as it is how we are designed to work with these earth suits we are in. The chakras are our internal energy guidance system.

Beliefs (aka FILTERS) block your chakras which in turn cause your multibody system to function at a lesser level than it is designed for.

ROOT: Red - Muladhara

The first chakra in Sanskrit is called Muladhara and it means foundation. It is located near the base of the spine. The color for this chakra is red and it helps ground you to the earth. It is here where family issues are stored and relates to feeling safe, loved and protected in a family unit.

This is the foundational chakra that relates to your feelings of security, mental stability, finances, and abundance. This is where root beliefs are stored. As you clear out your old beliefs (filters) this chakra opens up and spins. Think of this as you are busting up the faulty old foundation of your home so you can build a new solid foundation for your updated and remodeled dream home!

Muladhara is the chakra where physical diseases manifest from the emotional issues of the family unit because we feel unprotected and unloved by our "foundational" family. It is here where immune-related disorders are hiding out.

Imbalances in the root chakra are where the thoughts and/or actions based on a sense of lack live (i.e. overeating, hoarding, excessive spending or saving, etc.).

- When out of balance or closed off with filters, the symptoms include: fatigue, depression, emotional anger, low back pain, pain in legs down to feet. Emotional Symptoms: Feel ungrounded, unstable, unworthy, lack of self-esteem, flight or fight, isolation, and fear. Sexual issues that stem from energetic blockage or past traumas relating to family issues and our sense of place within a family unit as well as past life sexual issues.

SACRAL CHAKRA: Orange - Svadhisthana

Located under your navel in the lower belly, womb area. It represents emotions, sexuality/sensuality, creativity. This chakra is where your emotional filters are stored.

If you are struggling with your feelings look back to your root chakra when asking the why question. With the root chakra being the foundation of beliefs (thoughts), the answers to where the emotions/feelings (energy), were first created are found in the root/base chakra.

The sacral chakra is where our need to create the dynamics or control our physical environment with the requirement of relationships outside of the family unit. It is here where the shift from obeying family rules and authority allows us to explore and discover satisfying interests and relationships of our own. Svadhisthana is the seat and power of partnerships, as well as the creative exploration of relationships, sexuality, and life where we discover the power of choice.

This chakra is all about having the power to realize and utilize your talent to express the life you want to lead. A sacral chakra in distress can form/attract abusive, controlling relationships, and cause bullying in the workplace, fear of abandonment, and loss of financial, creative, and sexual power.

Svadhisthana is the seat of empowerment for the feminine energy within. It is here we also gauge the safety of expressing our feelings, and the foundation of sacred sexuality. It is the gateway to the divine feminine power we want to embody.

● When out of balance, the symptoms include: emotional instability, low sex drive, vaginal issues, menstrual issues, low back pain, sciatica, bowel issues.

● Emotional Symptoms: Feelings of low self-worth, guilt, shame, condemnation, self-talk abuse, discrediting oneself.

SOLAR PLEXUS: Yellow - Manipura

The seat of self-acceptance. Located right below the chest cavity - upper abdomen, your gut area. It is where the expression "gut instinct" comes from. It is the representation of personality and self-power. It relates to your intuition, your inner knowing, wisdom, creative truth, intellect. This chakra is where the filters of trust are stored.

Self-doubt and questioning come from this chakra. As you practice trusting yourself and what you are hearing and seeing, you remove the filters. You already know everything you will ever need to know; you are here to practice remembering and accessing what has been covered over.

This chakra is the seat of instinct and how you direct your life by it. Here you can look and see why you do what you do and see the correlation between thought and intuition and which one you are choosing to follow.

Manipura is all about honoring yourself, taking care of yourself, and forming an intuitive voice from your authentic self, which then becomes our natural source of guidance. How we feel about ourselves and self-acceptance determines our quality of life, how we are treated in relationships, in business, and in daily life. The Solar Plexus relates to personal growth and activating accepting of oneself and independent strength. One of the more challenging endeavors on this journey is to truly love and trust ourselves. It is here where our metabolism and digestion process occurs and our sympathetic nervous system is stimulated. Our sympathetic nervous system controls our flight or fight response. It increases muscle blood flow and tension, dilates pupils, accelerates heart rate and respiration, and increases perspiration and arterial blood pressure. When we have a weak or blocked Manipura we have low self-esteem and therefore attract relationships and occupational environments that reinforce or reflect this weakness.

• When out of balance, the symptoms include: anxiety, stomach issues, liver, gallbladder, immune disorders.

• Emotional Symptoms: trust issues, suspicion, fear of being wrong or doing the wrong thing.

HEART: Green - Anahata

The Anahata, also known as the heart chakra is the bridge between the three physical chakras and the three spiritual chakras, with it being the fourth seated chakra. By balancing and aligning the first three chakras, the fourth chakra is able to integrate and open. Thus, each wheel must spin simultaneously in order to remain in balance.

Anahata not only represents everything that involves love, compassion, and joy, but it is also the area where the love of Mother God lives and our three-fold heart flame resides. It's one of the most beautiful yet emotional chakras for people to tap into.

Located in the middle of the chest cavity it houses the Love flame of your I AM presence as well as the flames of Wisdom and Power.

This is the center of balance not only for your mind/thoughts but for your whole multi-body system. This is where your love center is literally. This chakra is where the filters around love are stored. Love for yourself, for others, from others as well as how you view love. This is the heart space of the Mother's Presence where divine love lives. In your new dream home and temple, you are building from within, this is "The heart of the home."

• When out of balance, the symptoms include: heart issues, circulatory issues, breathing issues.

• Emotional Symptoms: feeling small, unworthy, unloved, broken, deserted, and desperate.

• This is the seat of abandonment issues which in full truth is where the core perception against the Mothers Presence and divine love is located.

Stagnaticity is not being able to move past something -- look for the issue to stem from the heart chakra and you will find love as the only answer.

THROAT: Blue - Vishuddha

First of the spiritual chakras. This chakra is all about communication and how you show up in the world and express yourself. Are you in your power? What are you saying to yourself and the world? Truth in expression comes from this chakra. The filters over this chakra stem from not being in your power, feeling unable to speak your truth, to voice yourself, fear of ridicule for speaking out or up.

• When out of balance symptoms include: Throat issues, thyroid issues, neck, shoulder, arms, hands, fingers, sinus issues, and allergies.

When you are struggling with speaking your truth look back to the heart --- love is the answer.

THIRD EYE: Indigo - Anja

Anja is located in the middle of the forehead. It corresponds directly to the pineal gland. The pineal can be found in the center of the brain cavity in between the eyes and it is the size of a pea but shaped like a pine cone. Spirituality, the inner child, divine secrets, integrity, knowledge, and clear seeing, also known as clairvoyance are here.

The filters that cover up this chakra keep you from seeing clearly with spiritual truths, instead sees through perceptions. Healing your inner child helps to remove the filters. Other filters that are found here, are doubting your visions, and your instinct.

YCAL is the inner process of removing the matrix programming that has kept your I AM presence/Beloved/Grand Cosmic Being whichever name resonates with you, hidden beneath the hurt, pain, and confusion. Stuffed way down deep for protection from the duality matrix programming. As you are putting the puzzle pieces back together you will discover as your Inner Child heals and grows your I AM self is able to come forth that much more. The more light you let in and evolve the more you heal your inner child.

There are chemical substances that we have been putting into our body for years that are designed to calcify the pineal gland. This essentially closes it down and shuts us off from our clear seeing. The biggest offender is fluoride! Yes, the same fluoride found in the water back in the 50's and up for so-called better tooth care. In actuality, this was the same fluoride that Nazi Germany used in their camps -- Hitler knew. Fluoride calcifies the pineal gland. Fluoride stores in the pineal gland more than any other organ in the body and a calcified pineal gland is a closed pineal gland or third eye. Since it is part of your spiritual guidance system -- your sight has been like seeing through a keyhole.

This tiny organ regulates your daily and seasonal circadian rhythms, which is the sleep-wake patterns that determine your hormone levels, stress levels, and physical performance. This is also the organ that produces melatonin in your body. Melatonin is another thing that doctors and scientist have misled us on and you will start to see more information come forth about this. I find it interesting at how regulated it is and you can only get small amounts here in the United States. It is sold as a substance to help you sleep when, in fact, the truth is, sleep is a side effect of melatonin, not its main function. Melatonin holds a key to long life. I encourage you to do some research on your own and determine if it is something you want to take. I am not a medical doctor or a scientist, I will only speak from my own point of view and encourage you to do your own research.

• When out of balance or closed symptoms include: stress, being critical and too attached to logic, vision issues, frequent headaches, including migraines, insomnia, dizziness, overactive imagination creating situations that are not really there (not seeing the true picture or perspective) confusion, untrusting, feeling lost or spacey, judgmental.

CROWN -- Violet & White - Sahasrara (both colors represent this chakra)

This is your connection with higher consciousness, source and all that is. It represents unity, wisdom, purpose, and expansiveness. Awareness of what is sacred and freedom from limiting beliefs.

• When it is out of balance symptoms include: feeling disconnected from God, source. Cynical about all things spiritual. Feeling disconnected from oneself or others. Sensitivity to sound, light, heightened senses, agitation, feeling like you are on a spiritual merry go round.

You are learning how to balance the relationship between the mental body and the emotional body. You see, when you have this ancient understanding of how your mind and feelings are to work together, you then need to give permission to yourself to allow the sacred marriage to unfold. That marriage is sacred because it is the holy union, the gateway for your inner presence to come forth. Without discovering the root of the filters and clearing them then you are only doing a temporary clearing. This is why we have the back and forth so much. Because we are only clearing on one level of our multi-body system. This is a twofold attack approach. When you understand that the emotional filters, beliefs, and fears we hold onto manifest into physical issues within our bodies by way of dis-ease, pain, depression, and fatigue, coupled with the changes you are making by doing the YCAL protocol, then the energetic clearing of the chakras via mediation take place.

When doing chakra work you can incorporate the YCAL protocol into this to focus in on what is the root blocking your chakras. Talk to your cells and ask the following questions: **Why is this coming up? Whose voice is it? Where is this coming from? Show me the root cause.**

When we ask to be shown things know that your higher self can and will respond to you in various ways. One common way is through the tests, the things you resist. What you resist will persist and it persists for a purpose. Do not be surprised when it is coming to you in your emotional body, your feelings. Feeling irritated, sad, upset, frustration - those are clues for discovery and signs that you are out of balance and resisting. VIBE IT OUT first -- THEN -- get in alignment. When the thought forms that are showing up in your emotional body (feelings) know it is your answer and your test at the same time. ACE IT LIKE A MASTER -- BOSS IT BABY! Then go in and do more chakra work- meditate. Think of mediation like this - Meditate =Activate. So much energetic work takes place in the meditation state, now you meditate to activate the clearing, cleansing and activating the chakras.

TALKING TO YOUR CELLS

Each cell has two antennas one is broadcasting and one is receiving. TWO ANTENNAS ONE RECORDS ONE RECEIVES. Two transmitters --the way you think, the way you worry, the way you process. That comes from the playback of all that was recorded. One antenna sends out, the other antenna gives you feedback.... sensory cellular feedback. (sensory feedback...example: your sense of taste -I like that ice cream, I like chocolate cake.) Think of two antennas one that sends out what is in your feeling body, also known as the subconscious and one that receives the same energy you are broadcasting right back into your cells.

Everything your brain recorded during the first 7 years of your life, which was in the theta state, was programmed into your subconscious for you to refer back to in adulthood. So, by the time you are an adult your brain recorded everything you saw, felt, smelt, touched or heard. Your brain was in theta state which is the state where hypnosis takes place, this is where the duality programming first started within each of us. Everything we saw and heard was recorded and as they were being recorded the unconscious was creating filters for playback as an adult. Many of those programs are negative, disempowering and self-sabotaging, however, there are good filters as well. Think about it, everything you saw from the time you were born for the first seven years. Everything you saw as a child, everything you heard from your parents, teachers, outside sources turned into filters that were stored in your subconscious to be played back when you are an adult. How do they get played back? Well, they are played back through you. You start to run these different programs and filters; this how you react in life. Unless you disrupt the filters and make new ones, you are not going to see lasting change.

The power of life and death is in the tongue -- your words have the power to heal and the power to destroy, how you choose to use your words -- that is within your control. You are in the process of remembering this powerful truth. After all, we are a creator race on a 3rd dimension planet, and the 3rd dimension on any planet is the plane of demonstration. It is the plane where we demonstrate what we know. The plan was not to stay in the 3rd dimension this long, however, as free will beings, we created a glitch/loop in our perception that we were separated from source, love, each other, all that is.

For the first 2 Golden Ages we were living as our true authentic selves, then the fall from grace occurred and the glitch or loop in the matrix that was conceived by the human consciousness (not the divine consciousness) was created. The fall from Grace -- I am sure brings up within you some feelings or emotions of various kinds but let's bring some illumination to what it really is.

First, let's take a look at the word Grace and what it means. Grace is - The Mother's Heart, her Essence, her Presence. Grace is the greatest love of all. This separation we have felt all this time is a core perception that we are not good enough and need approval from something outside of us to just be us. The separation program in truth is only at play inside the Matrix. It is a perception of the mental and emotional bodies - in and of itself is the human creation. Grace is 144 qualities of love, comes to us from the Mother's Presence and has every quality of love within it. It has the Magdalene Force and every activity of the sacred fire as well as every light substance within it.

We were all born with a pure heart and feeling body, however, the moment when we are born into human bodies our mental and physical bodies are somewhat limited due to what we inherit biologically from our parents.

Our human body is biological and our spirit body is electric/light and it is stuffed inside our biological human body. Our spirit body knows everything but this was somewhat covered up when we came into embodiment each time. Essentially, we gave up our knowing for perceptions. Perceptions are formed through our internalizing of what we believe, what we think we saw and what we think we experienced, which may not be what you saw and experienced. They are inside of you, based on the internalization you have done and those beliefs and perceptions. Ask yourself -- Can you afford to internalize? NO -- everything you internalize escapes you. (remember the broadcasting tower analogy)

In truth, we are the human race, a creator race which is the individualization of Mother Father God who came here 15 million years ago. Our all knowing all love Christ Consciousness which is our natural consciousness, was traded in for perception when we unplugged and disconnected from GRACE. Conception is our divinity all knowingness all love. Perception is duality.

Human duality (consciousness) is in the mind. Christ consciousness is what you are inside of, your body is encompassed within it, and it goes out from you.

I am reminding you of these truths because I am painting a picture in this chapter so you can have visuals to attach these too. There is a lot to remember and as the veils are removed there are more and more things to remember and discover. The truth never changes it only expands and as you continue on this journey you will see more and more how amazingly everything works together and infinitely expands and all is one. It is human consciousness that keeps us stuck in thinking mode trying to figure it all out so we can have a perception. Perception is the replacement or covering over of knowing. If you struggle with trusting your knowing -- this is why. The more you question yourself the more you are leaning on your perceptions instead of your knowing - which creates the struggle.

Remember everything forms an image inside of you when you have thoughts and feelings together and this is what will act out in your experience. All the internalizing and visualizing both duality and polarity will have to act out in your experience. If you think about or internalize what can go wrong -- it will. It is not Murphy's law -- it is Universal law. Your feeling body is a magnet and internalization creates feelings. Our words have the power of life and death -- your own body is experiencing this -- it is the foundation of Your Cells Are Listening. Daily you are experiencing the truth of your own words on some level whether you realize it or not. Since words are so powerful, I would be doing you disfavor if I did not bring to your awareness a subtle matrix programming filter that runs in the background like a hidden virus whose sole purpose is to keep you stuck and questioning -- let's expose it right now.

It is the habit of words, what you say how you say it and the feelings behind the words. Many words that are habitual are matrix programmed which means when you pick these words or phrases up on your journey in life and use them you are activating the energy behind them and anchoring that into your feeling side of life as a decree. Yes, you can decree discord into your life -- that is what you have been doing when you speak, think or feel negative about yourself and others. One Consciousness -- what you do to yourself you do to others and what you do to others you do to yourself.

Here is a list of NO-GO words. No-go words are words that are designed to keep you tied to the past and rehearsing the curse so to speak. These words have millions of years of duality momentum behind them.

Have - keeps you looked into the past, i.e. "What you have to spend"

Try - keeps you in limbo -- never moving forward just staying there.

Poor thing -- this is a declaration over you or anyone else you put after poor. Keeps you tied to the matrix

Hate -- is a duality word and concept -- it is the anti-Christ (altered ego) -- a matrix programming designed to instill fear and discord into the human race. Behind it is fear, anger, jealousy, greed, lust, rage, murder and separation. The habit of saying " I hate that brand or I hate when that happens" -- (just for examples) you are binding in every cell of your body to the energy that word hate represents. It does not matter that you did not mean it in a literal way, the universe isn't here to decipher what you are "trying" to say -- it registers what you DO say.

Disappoint/Disappointment -- filled with judgment, shame, guilt, condemnation. Where did you feel it in your body when you read it? This word is heavy vibration that is an attack on your feeling body. Even something like "That movie was a disappointment" --

Frustration -- stops progress and thought processes - feel that word out, i.e. "I am so frustrated" --closes you off, shuts you down.

Want -- comes from the energy of lack

ACTION STEP: Make note of how your experiences change as you reframe your thoughts and words.

Facing oneself on the inner journey is not easy. Jesus said it best "the road is narrow and few find it" religion has given their perspective of what this means, but let me present to you a fuller understanding of his words. He was speaking about the inner journey, facing yourself and duality and remembering who you are and allowing your I AM presence to come forth just as he did. He mastered duality and showed us the way via the resurrection. His time here was not about the crucifixion as religion focuses on, no beautiful heart it was always about the resurrection. What does resurrection mean? It means to rise up and out of human duality. To have overcome the human battle of mind over emotions. Jesus overcame the world because he resurrected out of the human consciousness.

I challenge you to choose words that will redirect the energy to enhance your life not hinder it. Below are some examples of words you can use instead of the habit words.

NO GO	GO TO
Have	Willing
Try	Allowing
Poor	Blessed
Hate	Love
Disappointment	Opportunity
Frustrated	Peaceful
Want	Desire

Willing: willing is in the now. I.e. "I am willing to spend …."

Allowing: giving permission -- "I am allowing myself to do ……"

Blessed: reminder of the truth that only God is and no matter what is happening there is a blessing to find.

Love: the one law -- What you focus on expands

Opportunity: to find the positive/teaching moment/angle

Peaceful: brings strength, love, and understanding. "I am peaceful this situation will resolve itself."

Desire: comes from the heart, truth.

Speaking your truths in every opportunity you have builds momentum in the direction you want to go. It is creating your new habits, overwriting the old programming. Look at yourself and life in a way you never have before, and allow yourself the desire to all that you know you are. Do it in the divine way of individualization, put your spin on it. Do it in a way that makes sense to you. A way that fits you, that feels good to you and most importantly: it RESONATES with you. Meaning you feel that vibration.

I want to share a story with you about speaking your truth, and the power behind it especially once you have momentum behind you. After my healings took place and the radical body transformation happened, I had my normal yearly check up with my primary care Doctor, who was the same doctor who had prescribed to me the diabetes drug that took me out. She had not seen me since I was released from the hospital after the death. Which by the way is another whole story -- when I arrived at the hospital from the intake nurse to the nurse that was assigned to me -- they were so mean to me and didn't believe a word I said. The nurse assigned to me was a downright bitch and that is putting it mildly. Anyway as she was walking me to the restroom -- AFTER lecturing me that there are people who really need care and I should stop faking this "death" thing because I am too young for this (apparently I wasn't of the age to experience death) -- it happened again! I dropped on the floor and was leaving my body. Boy, did she change her tune quickly! When I was back in my room and they were trying to stabilize me, I point blank said -- I want that nurse out of here -- her attitude is NOT helping and her negativity and disbelief have NO place around me. Ok, back to my primary care doctor visit. She walks into the room took one look at me and started crying. She ran up and hugged me and was in total shock. Now, this doctor had been my primary for 10 years at this time and she had seen first-hand what I had gone through on this journey and her husband was the Chief of Staff at the hospital I was always taken to during my Lupus flare-ups - which was a frequent occurrence. She stated how good and healthy I looked and what was I doing. I shared my story with her and of course, she was in shock and a state of disbelief but didn't discount it. She then went into full doctor mode and got on with my checkup. I could feel she was in disbelief and that surely something was wrong medically for this to have happened. I could feel she was looking for cancer and thinking that must be what is going on. She does the breast exam and as she starts, she feels a lump and gets very concerned. She immediately makes a call to the hospital to see if they could take me in right away to be screened. She explained to me that during her examination she felt a lump and as she was continuing that she felt the lump getting bigger and wanted it screened as quickly as possible. I started laughing and said "Of course you found a lump, anything to discredit my work and what I have done will pop up. I looked her in the eye and said: "This lump is not my truth and it is only an appearance to discredit me." She replied that she too hope that is the case but with me, she isn't taking any chances. I was cracking up -- I knew this was a test. Off I go to the hospital for the urgent screening they set up for me. They do the images and they see something, so they call in a nurse who takes me to a room to do an ultrasound. Things are going fine at first until the nurse asks me some health questions based on what my chart stated. She was asking about how I lost the weight and why I am not taking any of the 21 medications I had previously been on. I was excited in telling her my story, however, she wasn't receiving it well. You see I live in the South -- hell I live in the belt buckle of the bible belt, and it is filled with judgments and criticism if you do not think the way they do. So now here is yet another nurse trying to put her doubt and perceptions onto me, well I was NOT having that. She continues with the ultrasound and I notice she is going back over this one spot. As she is doing this I am inwardly talking to my cells and directly to the lump that is illegally residing in my body. The nurse says to me that she needs to go get the doctor because she has never seen a lump grow as fast as this one was as she was doing the ultrasound. She had taken a few pictures of it and printed those off, as she was doing that I said "While you are getting the doctor I will talk to this lump because it has no right to be here. She laughed sarcastically and said, "You do that, do what you feel you need to and I will be back with the doctor, maybe he can talk some sense into you." She leaves the room and I go on talking to this lump -- this time out loud and commanding it to leave, it is only an appearance and has no legal right to be in my body. The nurse comes back in with the doctor who had a stern look on his face, and she continues with the ultrasound to show him what was happening and how she has never seen anything like it. The doctor is watching and she is frantically trying to find the lump that was growing in front of her eyes --after all she had the pictures that were now in the doctor's hand. The doctor asks her to move and to let him take over. He starts doing the ultrasound then does an examination then back to her pictures then back to the ultrasound. Eventually, he turns to me and says "I do not know what you did or how you did it and frankly I do not want to know, what I do know is there was a mass growing rapidly and now it is not there at all. All I see is a dense area of tissue that is not benign and most likely from your rapid weight loss. You are cancer free-- and I do not understand it. I know your doctor was very concerned as she should have been, but I want you to wait right here while I type up my findings so you can take this to her right now and we will see you again next year for your annual screening. Whatever you are doing keep it up, it is working." I turn to the nurse and smile and say "I told you, you didn't want to believe me." She was not happy with me one bit-- and I didn't give two shifts. I was ecstatic. The doctor comes back in and gives me my letter and wishes me well. As I leave the room the nurse was waiting for me outside and she was still a bit rough around the edges but she starts to apologize and say she is in shock and has never experienced anything like that and miracles only happen in the church to good people who do not sin. I could not hold myself back at this point, I started laughing and said "Well beautiful, maybe this is God's way of showing you how much more he is than your limited beliefs." "My truth is what I feel I make real." Do not let anyone stand in your way or tell you what your truths are. Only you get to decide that.

You are created unique; not a copycat robot. You are here to show the world your individual I AM Presence in full expression as you see fit! That means the plan for your life is for you to create it and live it how you want to, how it feels right and good to you. The only approval you need is your own. There is no one upstairs waiting for you to make a mistake and then make you feel bad or punish you for that mistake. THAT is the matrix programming you are desiring to break out of. Your Higher Mental body does not judge you, your I Am presence has never judged you, nor will it ever.

Your perceptions lead you to your experiences.

Your experiences did nothing more than fulfill your perceptions!

Understanding perceptions and your body are vital to radical manifestation. After all, let's face the truth we have all been talking to our cells our whole lives, and they have always been listening. They have ALWAYS been taking instruction and direction from you.

Now that you have a different perception of what is and has transpired in your life you can choose to make changes at any time. All you are changing are your own thoughts and beliefs ...aka perceptions, yet in changing how you see things you change your world. You are also discovering how to take all this knowledge you have and are gaining on a daily basis, and put it together in a way it makes sense to you so that you are being self-led on a consistent basis to your next unfolding. You are discovering there is a purpose in your pain and how to grow from it and use it to create your reality and help others along the way.

Picture a sunflower seed, it has a hard shell you have to crack open to get to the goods in the center. This is the same as your heart space. You have spent lifetimes growing that outer shell to protect your love center and now you are in the lifetime you have been dying to live and you have discovered the path to cracking that shell open to free your love or heart center again.

So now that the foundation has been laid the shell of the seed has started to crack which means more light and fresh energy get in and before you know it the shell has all fallen away, and what is left is the actual authentic seed that gives life. Not the outer protective shell that the world and you have known.

See your cells as that sunflower seed that has a crack in it. Every time you speak to your body you are clearing out the old protective negative shell that is written on your cells and you are literally changing the structure of your cells by your thoughts and feelings.

Action Steps: If you do not have a morning routine, today is the day to start one. Here are some suggestions for you to consider while you feel out what works best for you.

Upon waking before getting out of bed greet your I AM Presence and set the tone for the day -- qualify the energy and how it will go then listen to a meditation.

Stretch right after getting out of bed for a few moments and as you do greet your body starting at the cellular level and working your way out.

Greet your I AM presence, then spend a few moments in silence, just listening just being and set your intentions for the day.

Spend at least five minutes to 15 minutes talking with your body and directing it to only crave the foods and drinks that it needs this day to sustain itself at its best for optimal highest good purposes. *this can be done while going about your normal morning routine of getting ready* I do this while walking around in the morning getting ready, brushing my teeth, making coffee/tea etc.

Direct your body to crave foods it requires to repair itself today the quickest, healthiest and safest way for you. You have your body for the rest of the time you are here on earth, might as well start developing a bestie relationship with it don't ya think?

You now know you are not your mind, and you are not your body. You are the director of this play and you call the shots via your beliefs that are carried out via your cells.

By now you should have a good handle on the concept of Your Cells Are Listening and you have seen the proof of this working. Remember, your cells are ALWAYS listening and they do not judge your thoughts and feelings, they only act upon what you feed them. Your beliefs (thoughts + feelings) are the nutritional food you feed your cells.

As a special bonus for purchasing this book, I've included a snippet of my best-selling meditation Talking to Your Cells for Radical Transformation:

"I welcome my cells to reveal to me what needs to be removed from my cellular level regarding thoughts, feelings, and beliefs that no longer serve my highest good. I am allowing this change to come forth. I welcome these new changes and I am so grateful my body that you are listening to me and taking your direction from me. This way I will always know what is going to happen in my tomorrows, because it is what I am thinking, feeling, saying and doing today and you are on board with this and supporting me all the time. No matter what appearances are showing up for me today -- I know this is a process and I am on board.

- I AM HEALTH
- I AM WHOLE
- I AM WELL
- I AM AT THE PERFECT WEIGHT FOR ME
- I AM BEAUTIFUL
- I AM SMART
- I AM DEPENDABLE
- I AM SHOWING UP FOR MYSELF
- I AM MAKING DIVINE CHANGES
- I AM SO GRATEFUL

My body, I am allowing and creating the space for you to start the repair and healing process. I will show up for you every day and together we will go through the process and I rejoice because I know I am making the right choices for us.

My body, I will honor, cherish and protect you to the best of my ability. I will be aware and listen when you speak to me, and my promise to you, I will not stuff things down or ignore the uncomfortable feelings, no my body those days are over. Today I commit to you to face what comes up for me and to ask you the qualifying questions as I dig for the key that is always hiding under the uncomfortable emotions.

My body, I now know and understand that things come up not to harm me, but for me to acknowledge, heal and release.

I am allowing myself to consider a different perspective on everything.

My body, I love you and I thank you for always being on the job. As we go through today, I will remember to consult with you and to acknowledge you.

I LOVE YOU and I LOVE ME! I say YES to life and life says YES to me!"

You are a vast network of thoughts, emotions, and feelings -- this is by divine design and not by accident. You were not meant to go through life clueless and trying to figure it out and have reactionary responses. Not at all beautiful heart -- you were designed to know the future and to direct your life. There is no need for you to react to anything in your life. You now know that you are to know your future and you are to create and direct it. The following pages are some bonus materials I have included to jumpstart your transformation via Your Cells Are Listening. This is a lifestyle change and not a quick fix, even though you will notice things happening once you consciously start talking to your cells. Be ready for one wild ride unlike anything else you have ever experienced. To better prepare you for this ride let me share with you a few things I experienced after starting this.

The first thing I noticed after I first spoke to my cells was they listened and obeyed. The first thing I commanded to them in the days following my death experience was not to crave sugar anymore. The reason I did this is the diabetes drug the doctor had me on had given me horrible side effects and when I reported them to her she told me to keep taking it as they will subside, as you now know that didn't work out too well and what caused my death was a drop in blood pressure/low blood pressure (this is what I was feeling for some time. And I would feel like I was about to pass out). Anyway, I came back from the hospital and refused to take it again. I was now armed with ancient Ascended Master teachings and I was on a mission. The first thing I told my cells to do was to not crave sugar any longer, to make it repulsive to me. Later that day I tried to have something sweet and could not put it into my mouth. I would get the spoon up to my lips and my stomach would flip, now forgetting what I did earlier, (just keeping it real - I didn't expect it to be that fast) I stuck the spoon in my mouth and proceeded to eat my ice cream. That didn't last long -- I had to spit it out rather quickly -- my taste buds were not having it. Now here I am standing at the kitchen sink looking very perplexed as to why all of a sudden, I couldn't eat my favorite ice cream. Then it happened - out of the mouth of babes -- my son says matter of fact like-" Mom, what did you expect to happen, you told your body to make sweet stuff repulsive." It hit me like a ton of bricks -- I had actually forgotten that I did that and his reminder sent off all kinds of emotions within me. It was working! Holy Cannoli's! What to try next! This is how it started for me, so now here, I was not able to eat my go-to food -- ice cream -- what's next? I started grabbing things that were loaded with sugar and sure enough, I couldn't get any of it down. I then told my body to only crave the foods that it needed to heal itself and for optimal performance. This is where things got really interesting. I started craving foods I normally didn't eat and not healthy foods per se. There was an inner drive to find healthy alternatives for my go-to foods and ingredients. For example, the first thing I switched out was white sugar for coconut palm sugar. If you haven't tried this sugar yet -- I encourage you too and to do your own research on it.

I normally do not eat eggs so finding myself all of a sudden craving eggs-- fried eggs to be exact, and fried in bacon fat -- see I told you it wasn't health food I was craving - was bizarre to me but I went with it. I figured my body knew what it was doing and what it needed so I went with it. For the next three weeks, I craved a fried egg over medium with one strip of bacon and one slice of sourdough toast -- I ate this for breakfast, lunch, and dinner, and for snacks, I craved strawberries - just plain strawberries. All of a sudden, I couldn't drink milk anymore -- the sight of it made me nauseous. I never liked almonds or almond milk, but here I was all of a sudden craving almond milk and enjoying it. My husband and son watched all this going on and got into it as well. They started talking to their cells and their food profiles changed as well. We didn't judge any of it -- we just went with the flow and allowed our bodies to dictate what we ate and when. Through this process, the three of us have become mostly vegetarians and have changed our outlook on food and how our bodies utilize food. We discovered so much on this journey and every day is an adventure.

This is a small glimpse into this journey, so much has transpired in that past few years I could fill a few more books. My hope is what you have read within these pages has ignited a fire deep within you to test this out and make it your own. What do you have to lose except the old limiting ways that have been patterned in your life that carry the momentum of old energy?

To recap here is a list of things I lost when I started talking to my cells:

- Lupus
- Rheumatoid Arthritis
- Diabetes
- Cancer
- Lyme Disease and co-infections
- 67 lb. weight loss
- Body Transformation without diet, exercise or surgery
- Self-Doubt
- Fear

- Lack of Confidence

- Anger

- Frustration

- Childhood Trauma

- False Beliefs

- Perceptions

- Religious Bondage

NOW HERE IS WHAT I GAINED

- Self-Love

- Freedom

- Illumination

- Healing

- Rapid Manifestations

- Twin Flame

- Abundance

- Peace

- Harmony

- Balance in thoughts and emotions

- Taking my Power Back

- Health

- Amazing Tribe of like-minded hearts

- Found my way back to the Mother's Presence and The Heart of Go

ADDITIONAL ACTIONABLE STEPS TO HELP YOU ON YOUR CELLS ARE LISTENING JOURNEY

Here are 5 things you can do today to start you on your way:

1.   **Stop all judgment -- especially of yourself**

2.   **Start speaking all the things you like about yourself -- out loud to a mirror**

3.   **Find five things each day about yourself that you are thankful/grateful for**

4.   **Pick one area that you struggle with in liking about you -- take that one and make it your intent to change how you feel/see yourself in that area**

5.   **Apologize to your body for not knowing better and that you make a commitment to getting to know yourself and falling in LOVE with yourself**

No one can do this for you, only you can do this for YOU! Think of this new journey as the greatest gift you could give yourself.

Believe in yourself!! You CAN do this! I believe in you!

BONUS ACTION SECTION: FIRST BONUS

I want to help you put into action what you have learned in this book. I've included one of my power tools to help you immediately put in the work to shift. This is a challenge I have run in my private Facebook group - Your Cells Are Listening -- that has helped hundreds of people like yourself start to shift out of lack and allow abundance and change come in. Did you know that sometimes things are not showing up in your life simply because you are not on record accepting and allowing them to come in? Take my 30-day challenge and start to step into your new reality.

ACCEPTANCE JOURNAL 30 Day Challenge

I like to compare the awakening journey to being a tournament fighter. Do you have what it takes to face your toughest opponent -- yourself?

This challenge will help condition you to train for your title fight!

Before a big fight, every fighter knows they have to condition and train. A professional badass is not going to get in the ring unprepared.

My role as a Spiritual Mindset Master of punching fear in the face & kicking limitations in the butt is to provide you with the proper gear so you can take your training to the next level.

One of my power kicks in my arsenal of moves is to shift from negativity, lack, anger, frustration, low dense vibrations (which are all rooted back in fear) is to fight back every thought form that comes my way with one of my own that is designed to help me get clear, and to manifest what I want and NOT accept whatever I see as MY reality.

The Law of Life is this -- What you feel you make real. So, if you are feeling any of those denser vibrational emotions then you are going to attract more experiences to you of those same vibrations.

This is yourself (ego self) giving you (your authentic divine self) a cosmic ass kicking! All in the name of FEAR. False evidence appearing real. Yup...it's an illusion.

DISCLAIMER: NOW -- let me clarify here -- Remember, when I speak of FEAR, I am referring to the fear that we create within ourselves. Not the "your life is in danger" type of fear.

That power kick is this Acceptance Journal that you are now in possession of!

The road to radical transformation is like training for amateur boxing. It takes conditioning, strengthening, proper nutrition, training and a cosmic size amount of remarkable (radical) determination.

You have to stick with it and not give up or quit on yourself when it gets too uncomfortable, rough, scary or whatever else you tell yourself. Why? Because that is what you have ALWAYS done up until this point. QUIT ON YOURSELF. THAT is the exact reason you are reading this right now!

You have tried so many different things to manifest and change your life but it just isn't happening on the level you know it should be.

You keep telling yourself you can feel it -- the breakthrough is right there!

Yet you can't seem to get the results you see and hear others getting. What the Freddie is going on? Is what you are screaming inside.

Yes, I was there too! It sucked. Big time. It sucked SOOO much I was willing to do WHATEVER it took to change it. I spent A LOT of time and money on many different things trying to find the answer that would bring everything together for me so I could make it happen. That was AFTER I broke through my financial blocks (or so I thought) So why wasn't it happening? What is really going on?

Well, you didn't come across me by coincidence. Coincidence is not my reality, synchronicity is. You have been calling out for answers and the universe lead you here.

Synchronicity.

Now you are here and reading this so you can FINALLY get the gear you need to punch your own fears in the face whatever they may be for you.

Your goal is to radically transform your life FROM yourself& and what YOU have always done (face it) that obviously didn't work because if it had you would be over here on this side of FEAR with me enjoying the victory win. (stick with this and you WILL be)!

I earned this victory win! It was NOT handed to me no matter how it may look. I trained hard AF to get to where I am at today and now through my process YCAL I provide you the gear & guidance so you can take your training to the next level and help you skip the pitfalls that I found myself in.

What was my training? It was me learning to look inward for my answers and strength instead of outside of myself. I stood up and took full self-responsibility for me. Every part of it, and especially the dark shadow side. You know that side too -- we all have one. It's the side that we don't want anyone to peek into. We don't want anyone to know. It is our deepest fears -- our insecurities, doubts, hurts, jealousy, critical, judgmental side of us. You know that side you don't want anyone to think those things about you. Yeah-- that is your shadow self. It is the polarity to your authenticity.

Look down at the ground or on a wall on a sunny day -- what do you see -- ta da! Your shadow! Your authentic self is divine and it shines a light from within you so the more you remember who you are and bust through your limitations that light shines brighter and your shadow lessens.

The Challenge is a beautiful way to get to know yourself better AND to get clear on what you want and won't you will no longer accept.

ACCEPTANCE IS POWER --
Here is your opportunity to join me in my powerful process of
MASTER MINDSET SHIFT
These mindset shifts are known to cause:

TAKING YOUR POWER BACK
HEALING
CLARITY
MANIFESTING
RADICAL INNER KNOWING
FALLING IN LOVE WITH YOURSELF
HIDDEN BLOCKS TO BE REVEALED

This 30-day challenge is one of my personal process that I use for my radical transformations!

ALL THAT IS REQUIRED IS A 60 PAGE FRESH NEW JOURNAL AND A WHOLE LOT OF DETERMINATION TO CHANGE YOUR LIFE!

Are you ready?

Take the fresh new journal with at least 60 pages and at the front of the journal take the first page and at the top of the page write Day 1 and then the date. You will title it

I ACCEPT. then number the lines 1 - 8 (you don't HAVE to do 8 exactly)

On each one of the lines, you will write what you are choosing and willing to accept in your life as your new truth. EXAMPLE: I accept every means of abundance flowing into my life. Write down 6-12 things on the page that you are now accepting in your life.

At the end of the day before bed, (I like to do mine before or after dinner) you are going to open the journal from the back and take the last page of the journal and write on that what you wrong on the first back at the beginning of the journal DAY 1 and the date. You will title this page I NO LONGER ACCEPT ... then number the lines...you get the picture. Now on each line write out a statement of what you are no longer accepting that relates to what you wrote on the ACCEPTANCE side of the journal.

You will do this for 30 days. Remember you are in training young Jedi, be determined and make this a priority! This is designed to build upon itself and gain momentum. It is a journey, not a sprint.

BONUS ACTION SECTION: SECOND BONUS

Here are a few proven ways to start talking to your cells. These are my personal decrees that I have used on my journey and that I share with my clients.

Since everything at the core is energy, we can use the same principle of talking to your cells and turn that to Talking to all cells, here are a few examples of what I spoke.

To this glass of (   ) I speak only love, peace, joy, health, and healing into you. As you go into my body, you will soothe all areas within my body that are over-reactive, your intention and goal is to supply my body with your original flower of life blueprint design and cause no irritation or discomfort in the process. I thank you and I honor you.

Overactive nerves in my body (can use specific area) (OR whatever YOUR specific issue is) I speak to you now with love, compassion, understanding, and healing. You have been working so hard it is time that you rest and heal. Today, you will allow the repair of your cellular structure back to the original flower of life design your job is done and it is now time you return back to your calm state. I thank you for hearing my demand and command.

Emotional energy is the resonance of your core beliefs, whether you are aware of this or not. Resonance is vibrational energy.

To change the vibration from lower ego energies to higher God consciousness vibrations releasing affirmations are needed. Here are some that will help.

I open my life to seeing all that I have.

I open my life up to all the blessings and abundance God and the universe have for me daily.

I open my heart and mind to believing that all good in life comes to me.

Everything is always working out for my highest good. I do not worry.

FORMULAS FOR SHIFTING

- Acknowledge/ Accept/ Release
- Willingness/ Allowance/ Permission
- Recognize/ Accept/ Shift
- Discover/ Develop/ Empower
- Possibility/ Probability / Certainty
- I say Yes to Life and Life Says Yes to Me
- Allow it to be easy
- Stand / Face / Overcome
- Identify: Is it Useful or Useless?
- Qualify: Qualify your day before you get out of bed
- Qualify all energy you are allowing and accepting
- Set your Intention - Use your Attention
- Passion /Purpose / Desire
- Let go/ Let it flow / Energy loves forward motion
- Integrate/ Assimilate / Let it Be
- What I conceive, I can achieve
- What I feel, I make real

JUMP START YOUR TRANSFORMATION

I want to help you get the most out of this book so I have created this section as bullet point reminders - and quick things you can write on your mirror or wherever you need to, to remind you that this a journey and you must retrain your brain multiple times a day before this becomes your default. Stick with it and it will become your new normal

- **Believe you are worthy of the result you desire.**
- **Know that what you want is available to you.**
- **The result of your desire is SAFE for you.**
- **THE UNIVERSE RESPONDS TO THE MOST EMOTIONALLY CHARGED ENERGIES.**
- **If you have the desire and doubt going on inside you at the same time, you have split energy and split energy equals split results.**
- **You have the power to change your life**
- **For something to exist, it must first exist in your consciousness**
- **You project your consciousness**
- **Without intention, you are all over the place.**

ALL THE UNIVERSAL/COSMIC LAWS RESPOND TO 3
FORCES WITHIN US
CONSCIOUSNESS
ENERGY
INTENT

First rule of manifestation - Your Consciousness Creates Your Reality!!

Consciousness is a field of information that transcends time and space and projects information outward to create a response.

94

When you shift your consciousness - you shift **EVERYTHING** and changes are **QUICK!** — Shift into something **POSITIVE** — not negative and desperate.

What is consciousness?
Contrary to popular belief consciousness is not located in your brain or anywhere inside of you. You are inside of your consciousness. Your consciousness is essentially a quantum field around you that is made up of electrical, magnetic and light frequencies that are influenced based on

- **Perception of self, place, and power in the world**
- **Perception of the world**
- **Perception of your power**
- **How do others make you feel?**
- **Imagery**
- **How you picture/project**
- **Your beliefs - thoughts and feelings**

You also have two consciousnesses - one is human - the one you are very familiar with and have been operating from for lifetimes - the human consciousness - the little self. You also have the Christ Consciousness that you are working on bringing forth and being the "default" consciousness, you want to live from. Your higher consciousness.

- **Start practicing the Law of Visualization - What I conceive I can achieve!**

- **To make something real in your experience you first must create it in your mind, then add feelings to it then visualize.**

Visualize yourself and the process. **Visualize enjoying the process**. Visualization keeps items centered.

95

If you put it to the right or left, you can shift timing. To the right is the future, to the left is the past. Visualize yourself in the process, in the now. Be excited about the visualization — make it present.

Visualize the process! You can't only visualize the end and not the process and enjoying it — otherwise, it won't happen. You must add joy to the process.

If there is no peace and joy in the process for your end result - it is probably the wrong goal. Otherwise, you send out "resistance" energy.

** You MUST work the process DAILY!! **

The Universe will always serve you the most emotionally charged energy.

BREATHE DEEPLY and say to yourself internally:

I CAN MOVE FROM FUNKY TO FABULOUS!

I CAN MOVE FROM FEAR TO JOY!

Your INTENTION to move to a higher consciousness — is a SHIFT!

A fleeting negative thought will not change your destiny. **Don't get down on yourself for these**.

Your brain projects energy with every deep breath and deep breathing SHIFTS you instantly!

Your beliefs either give you POWER or TAKE it away!

If you have been hurt or angry — you carry that energy within you, so write about it, get it out and change your vibrations!

YOUR INTENTIONS ARE YOUR ORDER FORM TO THE UNIVERSE.

PURE INTENTION — whole heart, whole mind

Make a plan. Work your plan. Train yourself to be happy while working on your goals.

Do NOT move into desperation — this is the **Law of Paradoxical Intent** (self - contradictory). This will keep what you desire AWAY from you. Desperation and fear repel your desires.

BREATHE DEEPLY and say to yourself internally:

- **I OPEN MY HEART TO ALL THE POSITIVE THINGS IN MY LIFE**

- **I SAY YES TO LIFE AND LIFE SAYS YES TO ME!**

YOU ARE NEVER ALONE

At times on this journey, it can seem that you are all alone and no one hears you or understands you, that is nothing more than an appearance of old energy trying to put you back into fear so you will stop acting radical and play by the old rules. The truth is you are never alone you are encircled within a consciousness that is infinite, divine, omniscience, omnipotent, omnipresence with all that is. This includes the cosmic hierarchy that is here to assist us by guiding us, and if one allows master teachers in our lives, that can come close to us and work with us by helping us to remember who we are, why we are here and where we are going. They are all of the Light and they are helping those of the Light to awaken from the hypnotic spell that humanity has found itself in within The Matrix.

Who makes up the Grand Cosmic Beings of the Hierarchy? The Great Divine Director, Lord Melchizedek, Queen of Light, Lord Maitreya, Saint Germain, El Morya, The 13 Goddesses: Peace, Harmony, Purity, Light, Love, Liberty, Unity, Hope, Faith, Love, Charity, Justice, Music, The Archangels, Elohim, Eloah, The Elementals, Angels, Chohans, Lord Buddha, Quan Yin, Mighty Victory, Mother Mary, Princess Mary Magdalene, Emmanuel, Goddess Athena, Mother Mary, Grandmother Anna, Aries, Neptune, Helios, Virgo, Vesta, Luna/Goddess Diana, Goddess Venus, The Ascended Masters, Goddess Metamorphosis, Goddess of Manifestation, The fairy kingdom, The Crystal Kingdom, and The Plant Kingdom.

They have always been here waiting for us to remember them, to call them so they want to work with them to allow them to enter our space. Working with these amazing beings who I refer to as my friends, my entourage, the God Squad, but above all else, my family. We are all children of Mother Father God and we are all one family in the higher realms. In the Matrix separation and division are the family majors that are taught and played out, this is the foundation of what goes on in the third dimension. We are on a journey back to Oneness, and the Ascended Masters and The Cosmic Hierarchy are all here to love us and guide us through this process.

I encourage you to reach out and establish your own relationship with these amazing beings of light and love and allow them to illumine you with the forgotten wisdom that has been buried and covered over within you as you played on the stage of life.

During this Seventh Golden Age what has been hidden from us will be revealed, we are living in a time where exposure of the false must come into the light and be cleared. This means the ancient mysteries and myths you have heard about and wondered about are going to be revealed, first starting with us.

The Tree of Life teachings are alive and coming forth for those who seek its knowledge. This is the original Tree of God -- not the tree of knowledge of good and evil that the bible talks about. Where did Yeshu Ben Joseph (Jesus) go to for so many years? He was taken by Lord Maitreya to The Ancient Himalayan Mystery School where he was taught by various Grand Cosmic Beings how to be Jesus The Christ -- Emmanuel. He went to the mystery school to be taught what you are reading about in this book. How to be the master over matter, emotions and live a balanced life of love from your heart. He came to show the love of Mother God that many had forgotten and the path back to that love that we have not known since the fall from grace. Jesus was taught as a teenager being who he truly is while being in a human form. How to work with his "earth suit", his physical garment, his human form. Jesus along with all the other Ascended Masters and Great Cosmic Beings are making themselves known to those who are called for such a time as this. They are beings of pure love and light and nothing less than that can come from them. They will never tell you that you must do something, demand you do something or trick you into anything. They can strongly advise you to take to heart what they are saying or showing you but they will always honor your free will. Free will is why you must first move towards them, they are not here to be worshipped; they will be quick to tell you not to worship them - but to honor them as they are here to guide you. Honor them from your heart space and acknowledge them and they will turn their attention onto you and will hear your call to them. Most of them have had physical embodiments upon the earth and understand more than you realize what it is like to be human. That is why they are uniquely qualified to teach us and show us the way.

EPILOGUE

Beautiful heart the illusion always was the perception that it is one major overnight miracle: if you are good enough, loved enough, blessed enough...something enough THEN you would expect a miracle. That belief right there has kept you away from your miracle. The fear/belief you are not enough just as you are. If you got NOTHING else out of this book-- PLEASE PLEASE PLEASE -- I beg you take only this ---

YOU ARE ENOUGH

YOU CAN DO THIS

A miracle is a series of little events that lead up to a culmination of an outward manifestation of the inner work that has been taking place behind the scenes. So, you see - YOU are the miracle -YOU co-create the miracle. You know you don't have to wait around hoping and wishing your miracle to come to pass -- you know it HAS to because it is the universal law -- and that law does not judge the energy it just magnetizes it.

You have heard me say it a few times, but I am going to say it again. The way to radically manifesting my healing, life, body transformation, weight loss, my twin flame, abundance, finances, and the best of all this...freedom from the boxing match that was always playing out within me, freedom from being ruled by emotions and always reacting -- is to be irrational in your thinking, and feeling and cling to your new truth with all you have AND that truth MUST play out in your experiences. This is what you must do once you decide to talk to your cells -- hold on to your new truth -- even when the storms roll in.

With that said, let me remind you that you can start proving to yourself that this stuff is true and it works. You can gain momentum going in the right direction to help you once you have decided to do this and stay the course until you see the changes you desire. You can use what you learn as fuel for the fire to hit back ego and shadow with your new truths. You know now that ego and shadow have a purpose and a plan and it is based in duality so therefore it is a trapdoor waiting for you to fall back into it. Make no mistake about it beautiful heart shadow and altered ego are your fear-based consciousness and they know nothing else, you must hit back and push through the fear to get to the other delicious side. Your new lifestyle and miracle manifestations are waiting for you on the other side.

Thank you for allowing me into your heart space while you are on this journey of awakening to all that you are. My heart flame wish for you is that the words on these pages have inspired you to go within and face yourself in love, understanding, and grace and allow your true self to come forth. May you seek the Mother's Presence, the peace that surpasses all understanding and the love that you have been searching for. May they give you the courage to ask yourself the tough questions and allow yourself the freedom to seek with your heart what your truth is. There are many paths on this journey that lead to the same place, that being Source. I encourage you to seek the path that challenges you to be the best that you can be, that helps you grow daily, but most importantly, points you to the light and the love of All that is.

With Oceans of Love and Grace,

Denae Arias

ACKNOWLEDGMENTS

I have to start by thanking the two amazing men in my life, without both of them this book would not have happened. To my husband Sergio, for all the lonely nights, weekends, and early mornings that you gave up to make sure I had the space I needed to focus and make this a reality, I am infinitely grateful. The endless amount of encouragement, support and laughter were the ingredients I needed to keep showing up and doing a bit more each day and to keep stepping out of my comfort zone. This has been the strangest, most enjoyable on so many different and deep levels, journey I have ever been on! Thank you for not freaking out as you watched me die and come back, and then again when I went to bed a size 10 and woke up a size 6 and nothing fit. Thank you for laughing through it all and making me feel like this was all "normal". Your natural ability to laugh at the most amazing weirdness that which is our life is a precious gift that I treasure daily. You are my rock, my twin flame, my safety zone. You knew how to love me before I knew how to love myself, you showed me unconditional love and stood by me knowing going in, I was broken in many ways. Your love allowed me healing, truth, comfort, and strength to get up and keep going no matter what. I love you.

Nico, thank you for being you – just how you are is perfect. You are one amazing being and I look forward to seeing what you have in store for your future. I am proud to be your mom and what a journey it has been! Thank you for always saying it as you see it, especially when I wanted to quit and for believing in me, reminding me of my past victories when I needed to draw on something to keep me going as the hill seemed to get steeper. Thank you for your amazing graphic designs and branding, filming, photography, website, and insight – YCAL would not be what it is today without your ideas and talent.

Dawn, my sister from another mother, thank you for your unconditional love, endless proofing and editing, beautiful photography, and support. We've seen each other through some of the hardest times in each other's lives, and our friendship has been tested, but it stands stronger than ever. Thank you for believing in me and cheering me on and always loving me the way. I am no matter how weird and strange the experiences were. For always being down for the ride no matter where it is going, and for being there for me.

Jimmy and Lisa Tuten, thank you both for being in my life and allowing me to share my theories, experiences, trials and everything in between. I am honored to walk this journey with you both no matter what different paths we find ourselves exploring. I cherish our long conversations of sharing when we come together and how we are all growing and evolving and seeing the magic unfold in all of our lives. I look forward to what we will co-create in our future days.

Melissa Aubil you came into my life in divine timing and since day one you have been there with me just like in lifetimes past. We've experienced a lot of things together and its always an adventure when we get together that's for sure. I am honored to call you my friend, my sister, my bestie. You've taught me so many things that have been vital to my growth and to what YCAL is today. Thank you for your unconditional love, support, encouragement, and strength. Here's to just the beginning! Disneyland has nothing on our magical ride! Thank you for opening my eyes to the elemental kingdoms and the crystal kingdoms, your work with the star seeds, Pleiadians and energy is exciting and I look forward to collaborating with you. Your love has seen me through some of the most intense situations I have faced – thank you for being my rock and shield. I love you!

Lauren Marie- My spiritual daughter, thank you for allowing me into your space and help guide you on your path. Your wisdom, fire, and determination are a beautiful force to be reckoned with. Thank you for assisting me to take YCAL to the youth. You hold a special place in my heart and I am infinitely grateful for all you have shown me.

MaryBeth O'Dell – Thank you for trusting me to help guide you on your path. Your heart and your energy have brought such peace and a light into my life that I am very grateful for. Thank you for your support and encouragement that always came right on time!

LC – You have been with me since I started this awakening journey and have watched me grow and shrink and grow – here it is! I did it! Thank you for allowing me into your space and to assist you on your journey of healing and growth. Thank you for always being there and checking in on me when I've been quiet for too long. Your support has been the wind beneath my wings! Thank you!

Florence Machiedo – It was a pleasure working with you and watching you evolve, believe in yourself and take your power back was nothing short of magical and beautiful. Thank you for your encouragement and support.

Usa – Your kindness, support and friendship I cherish and I am so grateful for. Thank you for always showing up and just being you. Your influence and your life have touched my life in ways beyond measure and my life has not been the same since I first heard your voice on YouTube, and I am SO GRATEFUL for that and for your life experiences and you showing up has shown me it works. Thank you for being a living tangible example of the Presence.

Christine and Ian - Chris, your friendship and encouragement I value deeply. Our conversations are always so inspiring and keep me going. It is an honor to know both of you and to be walking this path together even though we live across the pond from one another.

The Rose Masters - Each one of you had touched my life in ways that I could have never imagined, and I am infinitely grateful. It is an honor to know each one of you. Thank you for helping me out of my comfort zone.

Radiant Rose Academy – The day I learned about this amazing place of spiritual learning, I was intrigued and I have never looked back. Thank you for creating the space for the Ancient Himalayan Mystery School teachings to come through and for being a place of freedom, love, light, and grace. It is refreshing to have a place to call home. I have grown leaps and bounds in the past few years being a student of the academy and I am so excited for what is in store. The teachings fill in the gaps and answers questions I have had on life and so much more! I am infinitely grateful for the academy and the student body as a whole.

For more information:

If you would like more information on my program The Immersion, or other ways you can work with me and go deeper, visit my website www.denaearias.com. While you are there, be sure to sign up for my Mission Metamorphosis email list and stay connected to further your healing and journey.

CPSIA information can be obtained
at www.ICGtesting.com
Printed in the USA
BVHW041356040622
638932BV00007B/33